EVEN AS GOD

EVEN AS GOD

Healing Relationships Biblically

Sermon in a book series
Volume 3

First Edition

ISBN: 978-0-9798844-8-1

All Scripture quotes are from the
Authorized Version of 1611.

Designed by Ken and Terri Lee McDonald
Cover photo used by permission from
www.shutterstock.com

www.kenmcdonaldfamily.com

Other Books

By

Ken McDonald B.D., Th.M.,

Here Comes The Bride

A critique of the Baptist Bride Heresy

Pursuit

One Man's Quest to Find God's Perfect Will for His Life

Defiled

The Spiritual Dangers of Alternative Medicine

Jesus, Talk To Me

Have you ever wanted to get God's attention?

(Sermon in a Book Series, Vol. 1)

Dealing With Bad In-Laws

A Bible study on Jacob and Laban

(Sermon in a Book Series, Vol. 2)

Good Vibrations

Overcoming Spasmodic Dysphonia
through vocal behavior exercises

Dedication

This book is dedicated to my dear wife, Terri Lee, who through the trials of the ministry, as well as the blessings, has not become bitter nor haughty, but has been a good soldier of our Lord Jesus Christ.

Table of Contents

Foreword....................................13

Introduction: Ever Been Hurt?....................15

1. Trespassed Against..............................27

2. Temptation......................................53

3. Rebuke..77

4. Repent..99

5. Forgive...123

6. Reconcile.......................................149

7. Proving...165

8. Salvation.......................................177

Foreword

Thank you for taking the time to read this book. I have a burden on my heart for those who, have done their best to love, provide, be a friend, and take care of others. Yet in spite of their selfless giving, they have had their heart broken for one reason or another. It is my desire to be a help to them in the writing of this little book.

I am not a professional counselor. I am an Evangelist who, with my wife, Terri, have traveled for the past twenty years ministering the word of God in churches wherever the Lord opens the door.

In those twenty years we have seen many things and experienced deep heartaches as well. Through all of the tears, as well as the joys, we have learned many things, and with the guidance of the word of God, I, would like to minister those things to you dear reader, by the writing of this book.

I mentioned that I am not a professional counselor, which I am not. Most of my counseling is done through sermons and writing. But after twenty years in Evangelism and a total of thirty five years in the ministry, there are some things that the Lord has shown me by personal experience and through the word of God.

As you read this book, please understand that I am not the authority. I am going to give you my opinion and knowledge of what the Lord has shown me, but my authority is equal to yours, namely the word of God. That authority is the King James Version of 1611. By making this claim I am reminding you the that the word of God states, "...let God be true, but every man a liar." (Rom. 3:4) It is God and His holy words that are the authority, not man and not me.

So as you read this small book examine it in light of the word of God and not in light of the author. I am only human, and what I have written is not what matters. What truly matters is, *"What saith the Lord?"*

Introduction
Ever Been Hurt?

Have you ever been hurt? I am not referring to a broken arm or leg, but in your heart. Have you ever had your heart broken? Or maybe your heart wasn't completely broken, but what somebody did or said hurt you in your heart.

Maybe you are a man and you're tough. You give it the stoic, stiff upper lip application so you can take it. But there has been many a man that will just "grin and bear it," yet when he is alone thoughts return for him to ponder. They are thoughts of a time, or of an event that broke his heart, and a lump forms in his throat, and there are some tears that trickle down his cheeks. Many a strong man has had someone in years gone by who has broken his heart.

I was talking to a Navajo man a few nights ago as we stood around a camp fire and felt the warmth of the fire in the chilly late night air. One of his many stories was about a man that he used to run around with. He said the man was very tough, a fighter that no one would challenge. He was tall, muscular, confident and a leader of men.

He lived next door to his mother and one day he went over to his mother's house. While he visited her she began to rebuke him telling him that he needed to get a job and be a proper father to his childen, and she was right. He had children by more than one woman even though he had never been married.

Upon hearing this rebuke from his mother, he walked out of her house, crossed the driveway to his house, went inside and hung himself. He could stand up to any man, but Momma was in his heart. Her words hit him harder than the fists of any man he had ever fought. Her words hit his heart. If it had been a man, the raging anger that rose up in him would have been released by fighting with his fists. He could not fight Momma and ran the wrong way.

Maybe you are a lady and you have had your heart broken. Maybe just the memory brings tears to your eyes. It's not shameful for you, a lady, to show your tears. There has been many a loving mother who rocked a son or daughter to sleep in their arms only to have them leave the home with no regard to their mothers' breaking heart. Years go by and that dear mother sits alone in her chair at home. At times she picks up a small dog or cat and rocks it in her arms, all the while remembering, as if it were just yesterday, when she rocked her baby to sleep. There she sits in silence with long tracks on her cheeks where the tears have run down and dropped to the floor.

Won't it be a glad day when we reach Heaven where there will be no more tears, neither sorrow nor crying, for the former things are passed away.

Today there are preachers' sermons, books, movies and talk shows that cover the subject of relationships, getting hurt, family fights and more. One of the reasons for the prevalence of this is that sin is increasing in the world. "And because iniquity shall abound, the love of many shall wax cold." (Matt. 24:12) The sinful actions of people are taking place on a greater and greater scale. The fear of the Lord is disappearing, and the love of self replaces it, and as it does people are getting betrayed, deserted, made fun of and on and on. Left in the wake of this ship of rebellion are multitudes of people who have been hurt.

What does that mean? Well, in order to get hurt you have to have opened your heart to love. And a loving heart is natural for an innocent little boy or innocent little girl to love their mother or father. It is a natural thing, yet many today are getting their heart broken before the age of five years old. Deserted, rejected, pushed away, abandoned and unwanted, they learn at an early age what it is like to be hurt. Many a little child has learned what it is like to cry and no one is there who even cares, all they get is a slap and "shut up!" All the child knows is the pain of being despised and rejected.

A beginning like that will make a person hard.

The following story is very similar to one that was told to me.

Years ago there was a young girl with light brown hair, bright eyes and with a lively personality. Her name was Desere' and she was about eight years old. Desere' had been raised by her aunt and uncle reluctantly for those eight years. They were not mean to her, and even though they had a certain impatience with her, it was all that Desere' had ever known. To her it was home.

She had never known her own mother. Desere' had never seen, or been with her one day in her life, but one Friday evening Desere' was told by her aunt that her mother was coming by tomorrow, and that she was going to spend the day with her.

Desere' was very excited and could hardly go to sleep that night. As she lay in bed that night, her thoughts raced as she said to herself, *"Tomorrow I'm going to meet my own mother. I wonder what she will look like?"*

The next morning a small blue car pulled up in front of the house. Desere's aunt then said to her, *"She's here. Go out and meet your mother."* It was strange though that her aunt and uncle never made a move to go see her, but Desere' was too excited to really notice. Excitedly she went out the door and down the cement steps and pathway to the street where the small blue car was.

In the car behind the steering wheel sat a woman. She was thin, wearing a red t-shirt, denim pants, sandals and had most of her hair simply pulled up in a bun on top of her head. A few of the loose hairs waved like the tentacles of an octopus trying to find something to grab ahold of.

Desere' opened the front door and nervously climbed in and onto the front seat. Their eyes met and her mother said , *"Hi, Desere"* to which Desere' replied, *"Hi....Mom."* There was bit of a hesitation in her voice before she said, *"Mom"* for Desere' was uncertain how or what to say. After all, she was only eight years old.

Her mom pulled away from the house and as they traveled down the road there was a bit of silence before her mother asked, *"Do you like to shop?" "Oh yes,"* Desere' replied.

Her mother then spoke up and said, *"I thought that we would go to the mall and spend some time shopping."* And so they went shopping together at the mall. A couple hours had gone by when her mother asked her if she was hungry and Desere' said that she was very hungry.

With all of the emotions of the morning, Desere' had become very hungry, so they got a bite to eat at the food court. Not long after finishing her lunch, her mother said that she wanted to go across town to a special shop. Upon leaving the mall, Desere' had to use the restroom. Her mother seemed a bit put out because of this and ignored her request to use the restroom. But a few miles down the road, Desere spoke up again and said, *"Mom, I really need to go to the restroom."*

It was like a switch had been flipped as her mother exploded in anger. She started yelling at her with words Desere' had never heard before as well as many she had. She pulled the car over to the side of the road while slamming on the brakes. With cars driving by and almost no shoulder on the side of the road for the car to park on, her mother screemed, *"Get out, get out, get out!"*

Desere' was now shaking and fearful, and opened the door and got out of the car. Standing on the side of the busy road, her mother drove off and to this day Desere' has never seen or heard from her since. Desere' was despised, rejected and hurt.

Maybe your story isn't that bad, yet some time in your life you were despised and rejected. Perhaps you enjoyed your mother or father's good favor, but there came a time when it was lost, and you became despised and rejected. Or maybe it was your husband or wife, but it was someone that you loved from the depths of your heart. Yes, that's it. Deep inside your heart is a wound that remains from that time your heart was broken by someone you dearly loved.

In the Bible there is a young man by the name of Jepthah, and he was the son of a harlot. A harlot is the same thing as a prostitute. He didn't ask to be born that way, he just was. The Bible says in Judges 11:2 ...they thrust out Jephthah, and said unto him, Thou shalt not inherit in our father's house; for thou *art* the son of a strange woman. His brothers thrust him out and he had to flee from them.

Then there is Joseph, who was favored by his father Jacob, but his brothers hated him. As

Joseph's brothers were feeding their flocks, Jacob told Joseph to go find them to see how they were doing.

> Gen. 37:18 And when they saw him afar off, even before he came near unto them, they conspired against him to slay him.
>
> Gen. 37:19 And they said one to another, Behold, this dreamer cometh.
>
> Gen. 37:20 Come now therefore, and let us slay him, and cast him into some pit, and we will say, Some evil beast hath devoured him: and we shall see what will become of his dreams.

They threw Joseph into a pit and left him for dead, yet God was with him. Some Midianites came by, picked him up out of the pit to sell him as a slave down in Egypt. Joseph was despised and rejected. Of course Joseph is one of the greatest pictures of Jesus Christ in the word of God.

The Bible says Jesus, "...came unto his own, and his own received him not." (John 1:11) "He is despised and rejected of men; a man of sorrows, and acquainted with grief." (Isa. 53:3) Jesus Christ knows what it is like to be despised and rejected.

Often times in our deepest hurts we think that there is no one who understands the hurt, or how we feel. I want you to know that Jesus Christ does understand what it feels like to be betrayed, despised and rejected. He knows what it is like to weep, for the Bible says that he is a man of sorrows and acquainted with grief. He was not a stranger to grief.

You may ask, *"Who is that?"* That is the Creator of the universe. He was born of the virgin Mary, became a man and was subject to like passions as you are. "...God was manifest in the flesh..." (1 Tim. 3:16) God became a man and was tempted in all points, just like you, yet without sin. He never failed the test.

The Bible says that, "...we have not an high priest which cannot be touched with the feeling of our infirmities; but was in all points tempted like as *we are, yet* without sin." (Heb. 4:15) The Lord Jesus Christ knows and understands what you are going through. And there are many others in this world who are going through, or have gone through the same thing as you, and they understand, too. "There hath no temptation taken you but such as is common to man..." (1Cor. 10:13)

Perhaps inside you want to ask, *"Well, if He is God then why doesn't he stop all the suffering? If He loves me, then why does He let things like this happen to me?"* Ah, friend, you are the answer to your own question. It is because of your suffering that you dare to ask a question of God. You see, one of the purposes of suffering is to cause people to seek God.

If you had all of the money that you wanted, and if you were in perfect health, and if you had no problems then you would not seek God and you wouldn't see your need for the Lord Jesus Christ. And what I am about to say is very hard, but it is the truth, and that is this.

There is a place called Hell, and God gave you a free will. You make your own choices. The Lord Jesus Christ does not force you to choose Him, He does not force you to repent and turn away from your sins. He does not force you to accept Him as your personal Saviour, but that is the ONLY way to escape the tormenting flames of Hell. Many a person has suffered in many different ways, but it has caused them to come to Jesus Christ and accept Him as their personal Saviour. Without the suffering they never would have gotten saved.

I can name four men right off the top of my head that knew their marriage was falling apart. They loved their wives and their hearts were breaking. In the process and from the feeling of helplessness, they went to Jesus Christ and asked Him to save them as well as restore their marriage. Of these four men, none of them had their marriage restored, but all four are now on their way to Heaven. One of those men said to me that he was glad that through it all he had been born again, but he still would like his wife back home with him.

Have you ever been hurt? Chances are the answer is, *"Yes!"* And maybe multiple times. Here is one more story I heard a preacher tell.

The night was now turning to the grey twilight before dawn. It wouldn't be too much longer, and the sun would rise to warm the frosty morning air there in the hills of North Carolina. A police car slowly cruised down the road. From the warm inside the two deputies peered through the glass windows, ever watchful for anything out of the norm. They were just outside of the main part of town, with houses, stores and gas stations interspersed between the open fields.

Slowly they cruised when their eyes did see something very out of the norm. On the right side of the road there was a little girl in pajamas. She was, maybe six years old, and standing there all by herself in the cold air. With her dainty cold hands she was gripping a chain link fence while she shivered in the cold morning air. Her light brown hair just touched her shoulders, was frizzy and unbrushed.

They pulled the patrol car just off the road and stopped. Not only were they concerned, but they were astonished at what they saw. As the officers walked up to her they could see dark shadows under her eyes and how she had been crying for a long time.

One of the officers tenderly hunkered down so he was eye level with her and then asked, *"Honey, what are you doing here?"* The little girl with teeth chattering a bit said, *"I don't think Momma is coming."* The officer then asked, *"Where is your Momma?"* The tender innocent little girl then said, *"Last night Momma told me to hold onto this fence and she would come back and get me after a while. I don't think Momma is coming."*

Have you been hurt? There is a way to get beyond your hurt and broken heart. That is the purpose of this book. Dear reader, your hurt will either defeat you or cause you to be a better person. But the victory is to be had only through the word of God and the Lord Jesus Christ. All you will be able to do in your power is to run from it with drugs, booze, sex, money or witchcraft. And none of those things will ever give you the real victory.

Chapter 1
Trespassed Against

> Luke 17:3 Take heed to yourselves: If thy brother trespass against thee, rebuke him; and if he repent, forgive him.
>
> Luke 17:4 And if he trespass against thee seven times in a day, and seven times in a day turn again to thee, saying, I repent; thou shalt forgive him.

The first thing that happens when a relationship is broken is that someone gets hurt. In other words they are trespassed against, which is how the word of God puts it.

If I remember correctly it was Christmas day about forty-five years ago. The morning had come and gone with us opening our presents. I know that sounds a bit anticlimactic, but that's how it was.

My brother and I were a bit bored so we decided to go hunting. We lived at 4000 feet elevation in the Sierra Nevada mountains of California and that year we had noticed large flocks of wild pigeons flying by our house. We lived in Twain Harte Valley subdivision, and it was nestled between two mountains. The small valley consisted of about forty houses that had been built where an old apple orchard had been, as well as a nine-hole golf course that was the overall size of an eighteen-hole golf course.

We found out that the normal habitation for the pigeons was along the coast of California, but since there had been huge wildfires the pigeons had changed their normal roosting and came up into the mountains.

My older brother and I grabbed our twelve-gauge shotguns, loaded them with high base, six shot shells and headed up to the mountain that was right behind our house. The hike to the top was maybe a mile, with houses only built half way up the side of the mountain. The top was empty brushy land, and oh, what a beautiful California view it had! You could see "as the crow flies" forty miles north, and nintey miles west. The sunsets were fantastic!

We took our places and waited for the pigeons to come. I hid behind a wall of volcanic lava rocks that I had simply built stacking them one on top of another. The dark grey rounded rocks were about the size of soccer balls. Orange and pale green lichen also grew where the sun would shine on the rocks.

The first flock of 200 to 300 pigeons came straight overhead and we fired our guns upon them. The boom of the shots echoed around the mountain and across valley down below. The smell of burnt gun powder was in the air, but we were lousy shots and didn't hit one of them.

Then the next group of about the same number flew by and we opened up on them again.

I happened to get one and it fell not far from me. Our dog Ginger, a lab/spaniel mix, retrieved the bird but took it to her master which was my brother. Then all of a sudden we heard someone yell at us. *"Hey! What are you doing on this property?"*

I took off through the brush having no idea where my brother headed for, but I knew he took off as well. Hidden in some heavy brush, my heart raced as fast as my thoughts. I had hunted there before and no one said anything, but I had no idea who owned the property.

After awhile of waiting nothing else happened. Then I heard more gunfire, but it wasn't my brother, it was a family that lived just over the mountain. They had come up there to shoot as well, and they merely were playing a joke on my brother and I. Whew!!! Was I relieved!

But I had feared that we would get in trouble for trespassing on the land. Yes, trespassing. What is that? It is intruding into and upon land that is owned by someone else, and you do not have the proper permission to be on it. To trespass is to cross over a barrier into or onto property that is owned by someone else.

In the word of God, a trespass is to cross over or break one of God's commandments. It is also known as sin. "If a soul commit a trespass, and sin through ignorance, in the holy things of the Lord..." (Lev. 5:15) Sin is more of a broader term, where trespass has the action of crossing over a forbidden barrier. When the barrier is crossed, the trespasser enters someone else's privacy, or place of authority. That place is owned by someone who has not given you permission to be there.

"If thy brother trespass against thee..." (Luke 17:3) Then the brother has crossed a barrier and into your privacy and upon what you own. Ownership is not always physical, nor does it always have a monetary value.

For instance, before marriage there is a moral boundary set by God. Inside that boundary is a place of purity, it is virgin, and it is very valuable. It is not to be crossed until marriage. Many today give permission for the barrier to be crossed before marriage, but that permission is without God's approval. Even when individual permission is granted between each person, they are still trespassing against each other's purity as well as trespassing against their Lord and Saviour Jesus Christ. I am so glad my wife and I waited until after we were married. We never trespassed against each other, and after we were married there was permission from God, thus no trespass ocurred.

While such a trespass may have the permission of both, most of the time a trespass is an unwelcome event. It is such an event that you are to rebuke them when they commit, or after they commit the trespass.

A saved man told me one day that some years earlier he had attended another church in the area. It was a small struggling church where the pastor and his wife were doing their best, but for one reason or another, the church was not doing well. Little by little the murmuring grew to the tipping point which took place one evening.

He told me the people set the pastor and his wife down on two chairs. Then the twenty or so people encircled them and as they walked around those two, they assailed them with accusations. Over and over insults, accusations, of where they failed, and other piercings of a sword, ("There is that speaketh like the piercings of a sword..." Prov. 12:18) were aimed and fired at the two in the center of the wicked circle. He said the pastor and his wife just sat there and cried. And then he told me that a few days afterward, he personally went to them and apologized for ever being a part of such a horrible act. That pastor and his wife had been horribly trespassed against. To that there is no doubt!

A friend of mine was instrumental in discipling me right after I was saved. He and his wife, though he was not a pastor, had the same thing happen in a pastor's office at church. Many of the people of the church sent stinging accusations at him and his wife. They, too, were trespassed against, and unfortunately they never darkened the doorway of another church.

Evangelist Jim White, who is now in glory, told the story of a church he was asked to preach in, but he was warned that they were in the middle of a big split. The members had trespassed so badly against each other that a policeman was required to be present in the service in order to keep the peace. Now that is pretty rough!

He said that he preached and tried to make them glad, but they wouldn't move. He tried to make them sad, but they wouldn't move. He tried to make them mad, but they wouldn't move. Finally, after three nights of the meeting, he stopped in the middle of his sermon, and asked the pastor who was sitting on the front row, *"What is the problem?"*

The pastor looked up from his writing in a notebook and said, *"It's the window coverings."* Half of the church wanted one color, and the other half wanted another color. So the pastor went out and bought a different color altogether and put them up, and the church was furious.

Jim White continued to preach, and after a few minutes he said something to the effect of, *"I think the whole bunch of you are headed for Hell. To be fighting over the color of the drapes."* That's when the policeman in the back of the church spoke up and said, *"You got that right, preacher!"*

A story like that sounds so stupid, until you find yourself in the middle of the same sort of situation.

Many a person was at one time in church, but no longer attends. Something happened where they were trespassed against and have never gone back to church.

No matter what the trouble, you have no excuse to quit church and thus quit on the Lord. You had better mark it down that if you do right, you are going to have trouble, and you are going to go through trouble where you are trespassed against. It does not give you an excuse to quit on Jesus Christ. It may just be the Lord testing you to see if you love Him as you ought. It is your love for Jesus Christ that will enable you to endure the trespasses against you.

Arguments arise within religions and when they do, look out! Wars have begun over differences of belief. Christians have been burnt at the stake for holding to the Bible instead of the teachings of "the church," as in Roman Catholicism or Greek Orthodox. Here are just a couple stories from Foxe's Book of Martyrs.

> About the year 1532:
>
> The next person that suffered in this reign was James Baynham, a reputable citizen in London, who had married the widow of a gentleman in the Temple. When chained to the stake he embraced the fagots, and said, "Oh, ye papists, behold! ye look for miracles; here now may you see a miracle; for in this fire I feel no more pain than if I were in bed; for

it is as sweet to me as a bed of roses." Thus he resigned his soul into the hands of his Redeemer.

In regards to Mr. Palmer:

He was tried on the fifteenth of July, 1556, together with one Thomas Askin, fellow prisoner. Askin and one John Guin had been sentenced the day before, and Mr. Palmer, on the fifteenth, was brought up for final judgment. Execution was ordered to follow the sentence, and at five o'clock in the same afternoon, at a place called the Sand-pits, these three martyrs were fastened to a stake. After devoutly praying together, they sung the Thirty-first Psalm.

When the fire was kindled, and it had seized their bodies, without an appearance of enduring pain, they continued to cry, "Lord Jesus, strengthen us! Lord Jesus receive our souls!" until animation was suspended and human suffering was past. It is remarkable, that, when their heads had fallen together in a mass as it were by the force of the flames, and the spectators thought Palmer as lifeless, his tongue and lips again moved, and were heard to pronounce the name of Jesus, to whom be glory and honor forever!

Even within Christian denominations there have been splits. That is why there are now the Southern Baptists, American Baptists, Northern Baptists, General Association of Regular Baptists, Primitive Baptists, Missionary Baptists, Independent Baptists, Bible Believing Baptists, Conservative Baptists, and I am sure more that I do not know of. All of these have some difference that caused them to separate from another group. It is the same way with Charismatics, Church of God, Four Square, Full Gospel, Nazarene, and many others. Division has been around for thousands of years.

It has been jokingly said that Abraham and Lot were the first Baptists. How do you know that? I know it because Abraham said to Lot, *"You go your way and I'll go mine!"*

The world comes along and says, *"See there! All that fighting I can do without. I want nothing to do with church."* But the world has had World War 1 and 2, Korean war, Viet Nam War, and hundreds of more wars.

Then there are the Democratic Party, and the Republican Party, the Libertarian, Conservative, Progressive, and Communist party. The world says we don't want to have a part in all that fighting in the church. You have more fighting outside of the church than the *"church"* has fighting in the church!

As long as there is sin, there is going to be fighting. But one day the Lord Jesus Christ is going to take all of the sin, and all of the unsaved sinners, and all of the fallen angels, and the Devil with all of his devils, and throw them into the lake of fire. The universe is going to be burned up and dissolved. The Bible says that the elements are going to melt with fervent heat. Then Jesus Christ is going to create a new heaven and a new earth, wherein dwelleth righteousness.

> Rev. 21:4 And God shall wipe away all tears from their eyes; and there shall be no more death, neither sorrow, nor crying, neither shall there be any more pain: for the former things are passed away.
>
> Rev. 21:5 And he that sat upon the throne said, Behold, I make all things new. And he said unto me, Write: for these words are true and faithful.

So there will come a day when all of the divisions, and fighting will cease, and the peace will last forever. That will be Heaven in deed! *"And they lived happily ever after..."*

But what about now? What about the fights that you have been in, where you have been trespassed against? Or the confrontations that you have been through where you have been hurt? There is a Biblical way for you to gain the victory over your broken heart and wounded spirit. Without the victory the pain that is there will more than likely ruin you and the quality of your life.

Maybe you have been trespassed against by

family. It's family that usually hurts you the most. It's family that catches you by surprise, and by the time you realize it your heart is broken.

Notice the following passage:

> Luke 12:51 Suppose ye that I am come to give peace on earth? I tell you, Nay; but rather division:
>
> Luke 12:52 For from henceforth there shall be five in one house divided, three against two, and two against three.
>
> Luke 12:53 The father shall be divided against the son, and the son against the father; the mother against the daughter, and the daughter against the mother; the mother in law against her daughter in law, and the daughter in law against her mother in law.

This is obviously within a family. It is a family with divisions in it. But you may say, *"I thought that because we are a Christian home that we should all get along."* Many a mother and father have suffered from an undue guilt, thinking that they had not been a proper mother or father, and because of it there is division in the home. They blame themselves when they have no reason to. They apologize over and over, hoping that it will restore unity to the family, yet it doesn't, and they end up bewildered and discouraged.

While I'm here mentioning the mother and father, let me cover that for a moment.

You just read in Luke 12:51 that Jesus Christ came to bring division. I had to stop, back up and read that verse five times before I believed it and made sure that I was reading it correctly. If you have to, go back and read those verses. Or get out your own King James 1611 Bible and read them in your own Bible, to make sure what you are reading is what I am quoting.

The belief of our time is that Jesus Christ came to bring peace, yet those verses are Jesus Christ himself stating that He came to bring division, and the division that He came to bring was in the home.

If you are a mother or father reading this book, let me ask you something. This will also apply to a son or daughter, which is everyone else who is reading this book. In Luke 12:51-53 the son and daughter are adults for they are married. If you treated Jesus Christ the way your son or daughter is treating, or has treated you, what kind of relationship would you have with Jesus Christ? Stop and think about that.

My wife had a lady, who was a mother, tell her one time that her son told her that when he was eighteen years old he is going to consider, *"You and father less than nothing."* Now if you told Jesus Christ that, what kind of relationship would you have? Would you have to repent and ask forgiveness to get your relationship back? You bet your booties you would!

There have been many a son and daughter that have been raised in a good solid Christian home and when they get out on their own, they don't want anyone to know who their parents are because they, the parents, are Christians. The children are embarrassed of their parents, and the way they live.

What kind of relationship would you have with Jesus Christ if He knew you didn't want anyone to know that you were a Christian? You may respond, *"Well, He just loves me."* Yes, if you are saved He does love you, but that does not mean you have a close relationship with Him, or He with you. Don't you know that Jesus Christ appreciates His children who introduce Him to others and say in an unreserved way, *"I am a Christian, and the Lord Jesus Christ is my Saviour."*

If your son or daughter was in a crowd with their friends and didn't have time for you, or pay attention to you, how would that make you feel? But if you were in a crowd and avoided any actions that would show that you are a born again Christian, what would that do to your relationship with Jesus Christ? No doubt it would be quenched!

And yet, mothers and fathers get treated poorly at times by children even though the word of God says to, "Honour thy father and thy mother." (Ex. 20:12) And this poor treatment is sometimes overlooked, or ignored by a mother or father, so as to keep the peace and to avoid any division in the family. What's more is that if it is brought up, and mother or father are hurt by the poor treatment, then they are often accused of being bitter or not right with God.

What is being implied, is that if you have been done wrong by your child, or children, that you are to act better than God. What? You are to go on as if all is well. After all, "Great peace have they which love thy law: and nothing shall offend them." (Psa. 119:165) The accusation is, *"Mom, or Dad? You are not right with God. You should freely forgive because that is how God forgives."*

The Bible has some things to say about this.

"And be ye kind one to another, tenderhearted, forgiving one another, even as God for Christ's sake hath forgiven you." (Eph. 4:32) You are to forgive one another, "even as God." Did you get that? Even as God! So how does God forgive? If you are born again, how did you get forgiven? The verse says that we are to forgive even as God, so God is our example of how to forgive. What is the procedure God put in place in order for you to get forgiven?

If your children have treated you poorly and have hurt you, what is the procedure you are to follow to obtain restoration? If your parents, or a parent, has treated you poorly, what is the procedure for restoration? If anyone has trespassed against you, what is the procedure to restore the relationship, and be brought back into fellowship with them? It is the same procedure that it takes for anyone saved or lost to get into, or back into fellowship with God.

To NOT follow this procedure, "even as God" means that you are expected to be better than God.

In so doing, what really will have to take place is that you will have to deny your Saviour and sin against Him in order to have peace in your home or in your relationship. But it won't be real peace. Real peace comes through obeying the word of God. There are no short cuts.

You see, there is a difference between forgiveness and reconciliation. They are not the same actions. I will explain the differences in the course of this little book. But what is often demanded of a mother and father, or someone who has been trespassed against, is to ignore the transgression and carry on as if it never happened.

Mothers are better at this than fathers. Mothers have more emotion and desire to have a happy loving time together. They often will avoid division at all costs, but for a father it is different.

There has been many a father who after his son or daughter has grown and left the home, has been transgressed against by them, and when they come home daddy isn't what he used to be. Daddy is distant, or removes himself from the family when they have all come home for Thanksgiving or Christmas. Daddy seems aloof and absent, for he knows that if he brought it up he would be considered juvenile and childish, yet daddy is right!

Perhaps the one or ones who trespassed against you say, *"You need to forgive and forget. It was some years ago, it is time to move on."* Many fathers will not do this, but neither does God. *"Can't we let bygones be bygones?"* Well, God doesn't, but He doesn't mope around either. Let me give you some examples.

God leads Israel out of Egypt and brings them up to the Promised Land. Israel, by the way, is a type of a Christian, since Egypt is a type of the world, the Passover lamb is a type of Jesus Christ, and the blood on the door posts is a picture of Calvary. The death Angel passes over when he sees the blood of the Lamb.

Not only is it a historical event that happened to the nation of Israel, but it also is a picture of your salvation. Israel in the wilderness, as well as entering the Promised Land are: "Now all these things happened unto them for ensamples: and they are written for our admonition, upon whom the ends of the world are come." (1Cor. 10:11)

So God leads Israel, a type of a Christian, out of Egypt and brings them up to the Promised Land. The spies bring back an evil report and Israel does not obey the Lord. So God leads them through the wilderness for forty years. Forty years later He brings them back to the same place and in so many words says, *"Are you ready now to go into the Promised Land?"* And they say, *"Yes, we are!"* Forty years later He is still dealing with them about the same thing.

Here is another one. With his mother's help, Jacob has disguised himself as his older brother Esau, and gone to his blind father in order to get his blessing. (In the Old Testament the blessing was very real and very valuable.) Isaac, Jacob's blind father, can only go by feel and hearing.

> Gen. 27:21 And Isaac said unto Jacob, Come near, I pray thee, that I may feel thee, my son, whether thou *be* my very son Esau or not.
>
> Gen. 27:22 And Jacob went near unto Isaac his father; and he felt him, and said, The voice *is* Jacob's voice, but the hands *are* the hands of Esau.
>
> Gen. 27:23 And he discerned him not, because his hands were hairy, as his brother Esau's hands: so he blessed him.
>
> Gen. 27:24 And he said, *Art* thou my very son Esau? And he said, I *am*.

Twenty years later Jacob is wrestling with an Angel which in reality is Jesus Christ. He wrestles with him all night and:

> Gen. 32:26 And he said, Let me go, for the day breaketh. And he said, I will not let thee go, except thou bless me.
>
> Gen. 32:27 And he said unto him, What *is* thy name? And he said, Jacob.

Did you notice the, "What is thy name?" God doesn't forget.

I know a couple who are missionaries. The husband told me one day of how, before he was saved, he was taking Kung Fu lessons. He told of going to competitions and watching other team mates focus Chi. Now he is saved and serving the

Lord Jesus Christ. He told me that there was a Kung Fu "doJo" in a small shopping center which he would pass each morning on his way to work. Each time he passed he thought to him self, *"You know, one of these days I ought to go in there."* As we were talking about the metaphysical workings of Kung Fu through Chi, and how it was contrary to the word of God, my wife asked him if he had ever repented of doing the Kung Fu? He stopped for a split second and then replied that he hadn't.

He told us some weeks later that after we left his house that day, he went into his bedroom and asked forgiveness for practicing Kung Fu. Ever since doing that, he no longer has any desire nor thought of going by the Kung Fu "doJo."

Yes, his sins were all forgiven when he got saved. No, he would not have gone to Hell if he had not done that. But there was something about shutting the door that he had opened, even though is was before he got saved.

This is merely an example. I am not saying that you have to confess all of your sins that you committed before you were saved in order to be right with God. Let me be clear, I am not saying that.

What I am illustrating, especially with regard to the sins after salvation, is that God does not let bygones be bygones. If you have grieved Him, or have quenched the Holy Spirit, or in some other way have sinned against Him, yes, you are still saved and washed in the blood if you have been born again. But your fellowship and walk with

Jesus Christ will never be what it ought to be until you repent, go to Him and confess it to Him.

Consider the following story.

In his early twenties Sam was attending Bible School. Called to preach a few years earlier, he was excited to be studying the Bible and preparing for the ministry. He had not grown up in a Christian home, but the Lord Jesus Christ had touched his heart with conviction, and Sam repented and asked Jesus Christ to forgive him of his sins.

Christmas was coming and his heart longed to go home and try to witness to his family. Closer and closer the day came, and finally school break arrived. Excitedly Sam found himself driving back home for Christmas. The closer he got the more excited he became, when something started to gnaw at him. The Holy Spirit was beginning to deal with him about something, but he wasn't quite sure what it was.

The closer he got to home, the stronger the Holy Spirit dealt with him. Then in a very clear way the Lord impressed upon, that while home with his family he was to apologize to his unsaved father for the way he had treated him.

Upon realizing what the Lord was leading him to do, he became surprised. Talking to the Lord in prayer while he was driving, and not too far from home by this time, he said, *"But Lord, it seems like he is the one that should be apologizing to me for the way he has treated me."* But the reply was very strong from the Lord, as He reiterated to him, *"You need to apologize to your father for the way that you have treated him."* Sam thus submitted to his Lord Jesus Christ and determined that he would apologize to his father while he was home.

He told me that Christmas day came and they had a great meal with Mom's cooking. Relatives were sitting around and talking. The presents had all been opened. Bellies were full and everyone was relaxing, but his father was not there. After the meal his father had slipped away down into the basement where he had a workshop. Sam knew that was the place where his father would be.

With his heart racing a bit, he got up and walked outside. Then walking around the front of the house, he descended the simple one car driveway to the small garage under the old house. The garage door was up, and he slowly entered the workshop. Kind of hidden in the back was a work bench. The florescent light was on, and in front of the bench was his father, sitting on a stool and hunched over, working on something.

As Sam walked over towards the bench, his father didn't even look up. He just kept working, seemingly intent on the task at hand.

There in the old, dusty, dingy workshop, with the aged rough-cut timbers that held up the house, Sam, looked at his father. He spoke up and said, *"Dad, I just wanted to come down here and ask you to please forgive me. Please forgive me for the way that I have treated you."*

Upon hearing this, his father stopped what he was doing. Then as if not sure he was hearing correctly, but knowing that he had, while still looking at the bench, and yet not seeing the bench, he said, *"I thought that I would never in my life hear those words."* Then with a look over to his son their eyes met, and Sam's father gently replied, *"I forgive you."*

Sam told me that joy sprang up in his soul, and ever since there has been peace in his soul, as well as with his father.

Sam never told me what he had done, but he was so glad and filled with joy that he now had made things right with his father. He was so glad that he listened to the Lord and did what God wanted him to do.

Mothers may overlook things for the sake of togetherness, but fathers will rarely do that, and God won't overlook it at all.

Thank God for the blood of Jesus Christ which covers it all, but if you still show an interest in your old sins, then you need to confess it before your Saviour in order to keep a close walk with the Lord. The Bible puts it this way,

> 1Cor. 11:31 For if we would judge ourselves, we should not be judged.
>
> 1Cor. 11:32 But when we are judged, we are chastened of the Lord, that we should not be condemned with the world.

Have you been trespassed against? Now when I ask this you need to determine if it was a legitimate trespass. Some people get upset over the slightest things, but was it a legitimate trespass? Was it something that actually broke your heart?

The Bible says: And above all things have fervent charity among yourselves: for charity shall cover the multitude of sins. (1Pet. 4:8)

Charity will enable you to look past the sins of others, and there is a need for this. Was the person a new babe in the Lord and didn't know any better? All I am saying is make sure that it is a legitimate trespass. If you are not sure then ask the Lord in prayer.

I was preaching a meeting one time in my home church, where we had been members for over seven years. The meeting was going well, with hearts seeming to be touched by the Spirit of God each night. It was scheduled to be a Sunday-through-Sunday meeting.

As I usually try to do, I went to prayer on Friday afternoon for the service that night and prayed for direction as to what the Lord would have me to preach. I will usually pray for an hour or so before each meeting. The Lord seemed to impress upon me to preach on a subject that I had preached on in a number of churches, but one which was a bit pointed and controversial. I preached on the subject of the dangers of New Age medicine.

It seemed to go very well. Though I do not preach to please man, yet it is a joy when people tell you that they got a blessing, or that the Lord dealt with them from the sermon I preached. That night over 90 percent of the small thirty or so person congregation came up to me and told me that they had got a blessing, and thanked me for preaching the sermon. One of the members gave me money towards the writing of a book on the subject of the dangers of New Age medicine, which I have now written. From all I could tell it went well, though the pastor seemed a bit agitated.

The next night, which was Saturday, there was no service, but my wife and I were called into the pastor's office at around 10:00 P.M. This was my pastor at the time, and he proceeded to rebuke me for preaching the sermon. I was completely caught off guard and amazed at what was happening. I will not go into the details, but he was upset. I asked for Scripture to show where I was wrong, but he gave none. Nevertheless, I am not out to cause trouble in a church, much less my own home church.

Though I did not have a legitimate reason to apologize, yet I was troubled that my pastor was so upset, so I did apologize to him about what I had done. This had no effect, as there was obviously no forgiveness reciprocated to me. We were told to get off the property and were not allowed to attend the services of the church. (I still wonder why he included my wife as she had done nothing and was a member of the church.)

Did he have a complaint about me and what I had done? Certainly! Was it a legitimate complaint? No! He had no Scripture to show what I had done wrong, nor was he even reasonable after I apologized to him.

Did I trespass against him? Not at all, for in the sermon I never aimed at anyone. I covered the subject and showed from the word of God where it was wrong for a child of God to use that medicine.

I had preached the same sermon just two weeks earlier in a church, and I had absolutely no idea what was going on in the church. When I was finished, the pastor got up and apologized to his people for recommending the New Age medicine to them. That is the right response, and that church has grown since that meeting.

If you live for the Lord Jesus Christ, whether you are a preacher or not, there will be times that you make other people mad. It is not because you have trespassed against them, it is because they are not living right and are being convicted by the word of God.

There is one thing for sure though and it is that we continually, trespass against the Creator of the universe, the Lord Jesus Christ. He is offended by it, and if we are saved it hinders our relationship with Him until we confess it to Him. Yes, if we are saved, He does still love us. He will never leave us nor forsake us.

Your standing in Jesus Christ will never change. It was settled the moment that you were born again, washed in the blood of Christ, and regenerated by the Spirit of God. There are a number of things that took place the very moment that you were born again, and they will never change no matter how you live. That has to do with your standing, but what I am writing about and dealing with right now has to do with your state.

What is your spiritual state? Are you in fellowship with Jesus Christ? Are there sins that are hindering your walk with the Lord Jesus Christ? Are there idols in your heart? Have you trespassed against your Saviour and never repented of it? Are there sins that you have never confessed and asked Him to forgive? If so, then your fellowship with Jesus Christ is not what it ought to be.

You may ask, *"But what about grace?"* The Bible states that we are not under the law but under grace, and "Where no law is, *there is* no transgression." (Rom. 4:15) That is true in regard to your standing, but the Bible also says: "For, brethren, ye have been called unto liberty; only *use* not liberty for an occasion to the flesh, but by love serve one another." (Gal. 5:13) You are not to use liberty for an occasion to the flesh. Yes, you are under grace but the Bible says:

> "For there are certain men crept in unawares, who were before of old ordained to this condemnation, ungodly men, turning the grace of our God into lasciviousness, and denying the only Lord God, and our Lord Jesus Christ." (Jude 4)

You can take your liberty and grace, and end up in lasciviousness, which are vulgar, base and rude actions. Many Christians today are doing this.

Just watch the Contemporary Christian music performances-well, on second thought, don't!

Modern Christianity has gotten to the point where there is little to no difference between it and the world. I heard a story recently of a man who had gotten saved and came out of the Death Metal music. He had been a guitarist in a band. Now that he is saved, he told his pastor that he is having trouble when he goes to church and listens to the Contemporary Christian music because the devils he experienced in the Death Metal music are the same ones that he is sensing in the contemporary Christian music. Lasciviousness! It is a trespass against our Lord Jesus Christ and will destroy your walk with God.

In this study on forgiveness and reconciliation the first element of it all is that there is a legitimate trespass. "If thy brother trespass against thee." (Luke 17:3) Trespass happens with family as well with friends, and if you did to Jesus Christ what happened to you, what kind of relationship would you have with Him?

Chapter 2
Temptation

When you have been trespassed against, often times it surprises you because of the one who is trespassing against you. The word of God says, "If thy brother trespass against thee." (Luke 17:3) It is someone you know and chances are, it is someone that you love. This being the case, then it catches you off guard. You don't guard yourself when you are around the ones you love and trust.

With your guard down you are vulnerable. You are vulnerable to be hurt in your heart, for it is from your heart that you love. This surprise "attack" reaches its mark and cuts open your heart and leaves it bleeding. Your surprise then fades away, and you feel the pain the trespass has left, with your heart wounded and bleeding.

The wound becomes worse if you forget the following verse:

> For we wrestle not against flesh and blood, but against principalities, against powers, against the rulers of the darkness of this world, against spiritual wickedness in high *places*. (Eph. 6:12)

You have just been attacked by surprise and the fiery dart reached its mark. Did your loved one, or your close friend intend on hurting you? I doubt it! Nevertheless that is what happened.

Your surprise turns to pain, and your pain turns to anger, and your anger can turn into bitterness if you do not follow what the word of God says for you to do. If your anger turns to bitterness, then the spiritual wickedness in high places has won that battle.

Bitterness turns you hard and unable to love as God would have you to. If it goes that far, and with many it does, then you have lost the battle. Because of your pride, your walls go up and you sit alone in your self-made prison, claiming to yourself, *"I am safe in here, and no one can hurt me."* But that is not God's will for your life, and in such a case a Christian is not right with their Saviour Jesus Christ. Your fellowship with Him is severely broken.

There are going to be things in this life that you receive that you do not deserve. Whether you receive them through loved ones or not, let me stress again that, events are going to take place in your life that you do not deserve and how you react to them depends on what you were the day before they happen to you.

A correct response is only born out of a correct walk with Jesus Christ. That being said though, there are things that happen in this life that are bitter. Have you ever eaten something that is bitter? I mean really bitter. If you have, then you will never forget it. It is something that stands out in your memory.

There was a time when I lived in the hills of California. It was the Sierra Nevada mountains, and this time we were living at about 3500-feet elevation. At that elevation there is a bush that grows commonly known as poison oak, and I am very allergic to it. At 4000-feet elevation it will not grow, because it stops growing at, around 3800-feet. Well, it was growing all around on the hillside where we had just moved into a new home. I made doubly sure that I stayed away from it as we moved in, but in the process of time I decided that it was necessary to eradicate it from my property. After having my dog and cat walk through it and then coming in the house and rubbing against me I ended up getting the itchy rash. I hate that itchy rash!

My only relief for the itch was to scratch it until it bled and then pour alcohol on it and let it sting and burn at the same time. Then I would get in the shower and put as hot as I could stand water on it, wash with soap and rinse off with cold water. That would give me four hours relief from the itch.

Well, I decided to remove it from my yard.

Clothed in long sleeves with rubber bands around the cuffs, boots covered by denim work pants, hat, gloves, and extreme caution, I proceeded to prune back the bushes without touching them. But, in spite of all of the precautions, I broke out all over my body in poison oak and I was miserable.

Upon entering the local drug store I met a man whom I had known for decades, and we said a cordial hello. He asked what I was doing and I had one thing on my mind which was to try to get some relief from the itching.

Trying to be a help, he then said to me that the Indians used to suck on wild peach leaves in order to build up their immunity to poison oak. He then showed me these two-feet high, single stem, dark green-leaved plants that were growing on the hillside. He pointed to them and said, *"Get you some of them and suck on 'em. You'll build up your immunity and it will relieve the itching."*

This sounded to me like a message from Heaven. It was free and my problems would be solved. So I went over to the bank by the road upon which these plants were growing and picked a pretty good bunch of wild peach leaves.

I brought them home and washed them off. Then with my wife, son and daughter watching, I took one of those leaves, and seeing they were fairly long and narrow, I rolled it up and put it in my mouth. Then I chomped down on it, starting to suck on the leaf. Immediately I was made aware of what it's like to eat something that is very bitter. Oh, was that ever bitter!!!

My teeth turned green from the juice of the leaves mixing with my saliva. Little pieces of leaf stuck to the inside of my cheeks as my teeth broke it up. Then with a swipe of my finger, I removed what I could and placed another rolled up leaf in my mouth and chomped down again. Oh, was that ever bitter!!!

I don't know if wild peach leaves work to gain an immunity against poison oak, because it didn't take long and I decided I would go to the doctor and be treated. I am so glad that I did! But those leaves were bitter, and I will never forget it.

We live in a sinful world, and in this sinful world there are going to be things happening to you that are not fun. Actually they are quite bitter. There are going to be things happening in this world that you do not deserve. Bad is going to come your way that you do not deserve. At least that is how it will seem.

I am not trying to be hard, please understand that. But if you and I got what we deserved, we would be in a place called Hell suffering in flames of fire. That is what you deserve, and that is what I deserve. Remembering this can ease the pain of the bitter events of your life.

Well, anyway, there are going to be things happening to you that you did not ask for, you did not earn, and maybe even you tried to avoid. The old timers had a much more realistic view of life and death. Death was much more real to people in the years gone by.

Notice the following epitaphs.

Wyoming County, New York
She was in health at 11:30 A.M.
And left for Heaven at 3:30 P.M.

Plymouth, Massachusets
On the tombstone of a babe of four days old

Since I so very soon was done for
I wonder what I was begun for.

Orange County, New York

Listen, Mother, Aunt and me
Were killed, here we be
We should not had time to missle
Had they blown the engine whistle

That is just a few examples of bitter deaths happening to some people. It leaves you wondering what it was that caused such things to happen? And for the survivors, I wonder how they reacted to the bitter news?

In these cases one would be turned straight to God, as it was a matter of death. But for you, maybe it was a loved one who trespassed against you, and it left a very bitter taste in your mouth, so to speak. You didn't deserve it but it came to you anyway. A temptation is now set before you. You can either become bitter or can allow it, by the grace of God, to make you better. It will take work, but it can make you better.

May I remind you of a story that took place some two thousand years ago in a place called Calvary. There on a rugged wooden cross the Holy Son of God, Jesus Christ, was crucified. In the physical sense He was condemned as guilty, even though Pilate said, *"I find no fault in this man."* He was numbered with the transgressors, yet He was innocent. Jesus Christ did not deserve to die on the cross. He received bad that he did not deserve.

Spiritually as well, Jesus Christ did not deserve to die. He was God manifest in the flesh. He had never sinned one time, yet He was crucified and shed His blood to pay for my sins and your sins. His death is the greatest picture of love that ever will be.

If you have received bad that you do not deserve, then look to the Cross and behold the Lamb of God being tortured, bleeding and dying when He did not deserve it either. You can go to Him and tell Him all about your trouble and He understands. He will not laugh at you, mock you or put you off. He will wrap His arms around you, comfort you and help you through your valley.

As I have stated that you may receive bad that you do not deserve, conversely you may not receive good that you do deserve. Perhaps you have labored with a loved one in their sickness. You were there to help them when no one else would help. Yet when they passed away you were ignored, and those who could have cared less end up with the inheritance.

Here is an example of not receiving good that you deserve. This is copied from a Facebook page titled *Grandparents Denied Access To Grandchildren*:

> I am a grandmother who is not able to have access to my grandchildren because of a fall out with my daughter. Looked after Samuel from 7 weeks, and was suddenly denied access almost two years ago. Samuel and Sarah we love you so very much and always will. Hope when you are older Samuel you will come to see us. Pray every night for this.
>
> (https://www.facebook.com/Grandparents-denied-access-to-grandchildren-380075265394948/#)

I could go on and on with examples, but there are going to be times in life when you are not appreciated for the labor that you have put in. There will be times when you do not receive the good that you deserve and it can make you bitter, or it can make you better. The choice is yours. This book will show you the steps to get beyond defeat, and thus gain the victory. Don't let what has happened to you destroy you, for that is not God's will for your life.

Up to this point I have written about what has happened to you, but now I am going to write about what you must do to get the victory. This first step is very important in your gaining the victory.

Why? Because it is going to give you a half step

up. The first step without it would be too high to properly climb. This is a half step that will help you climb out of the possible trap that you lay in. I am going to start with a story from the Bible, and I will freely tell it.

Israel has just seen God do a great miracle which saved their lives. Moses lifted up his rod over the Red Sea and the waters parted. Israel went through the sea on dry ground. The waters were a wall to them on the right and the left. Pharaoh with all of his chariots came after them and God closed the waters upon Pharaoh and drowned Pharaoh and all of his army.

(The wreckage of Pharaoh's army has been found under the Red Sea. You can see pictures of it if you search YouTube and type in Red Sea Crossing, Jonathan Gray or Ron Wyatt. In my meetings I sell a DVD titled The Exodus Revealed.)

After Israel came out on the other side of the Red Sea they sang and danced on the banks of the sea. Then just three days later they were thirsty and came to some waters to drink, but they could not because the waters were very bitter. If they would have drank from those waters it would have killed them. So too, if you drink from, or continue to drink your bitter waters, they will kill you.

The people of Israel began to cry out to Moses saying, *"What shall we drink?"* Moses then went to prayer to God and asked Him what he should do? God showed him a tree, and when Moses cast the tree into the waters then the waters were made sweet. The Israelites not only were able to drink of them, but the waters were enjoyable to drink. The waters were made sweet. (Ex. 15:25)

I don't know what has happened to you, but I do know that with the help of God your bitter waters can be made sweet, so that instead of them being painful and deadly, they can become sweet and a joy to drink. "With God all things are possible." (Matt. 19:26) Your tears of pain can be turned into smiles of joy. Perhaps you scoff and question how could this be? God is able if you will trust Him. I didn't say your will would be done, I said He can make your bitter waters sweet.

There is a tree that you can put into the waters, and it is the tree known as Calvary. It is the Cross upon which the Lord Jesus Christ died. Your life's "bitter waters" can be made sweet when you put the cross into the midst of them. You see, at the heart of the cross is forgiveness. The cross is the only place sinful man can go to be forgiven by God. There is no other place to go.

When I view the cross, I see the Lord Jesus Christ being crucified. Right at the beginning of his crucifixion, about 9:15 a.m., Jesus Christ speaks, "...Father, forgive them; for they know not what they do." (Luke 23:34)

Now, before you jump to any conclusions hear me out. The first step in getting victory over your bitterness will require forgiveness, but it probably is not the way you are thinking.

> "21 Then came Peter to him, and said, Lord, how oft shall my brother sin against

me, and I forgive him? till seven times?

22 Jesus saith unto him, I say not unto thee, Until seven times: but, Until seventy times seven." (Matt. 18:21-22)

It is God's will for you to forgive, but this is what I call vertical forgiveness. This forgiveness is not in order to restore a relationship. This forgiveness is in order to not become bitter and subsequently lose you walk and fellowship with God. Bitterness grieves God.

> 30 And grieve not the holy Spirit of God, whereby ye are sealed unto the day of redemption.
>
> 31 Let all bitterness, and wrath, and anger, and clamour, and evil speaking, be put away from you, with all malice. (Eph. 4:30-31)

All those qualities mentioned in verse 31 grieve the Holy Spirit, and they are all a result of bitterness. Forgiveness before God is what you must do, and there is a way to do this. The only thing that makes forgiveness hard to do is pride.

I was preaching a meeting years ago in a small country church. It was a Sunday through Wednesday meeting, and Sunday evening I preached on bitterness. I covered what I am covering now in this book, which was that if someone had done you wrong, then you must forgive them. Not to restore a relationship, but to stay right with God. Not only that, but if you have been bitter in your heart toward this person that trespassed against you, then you contact them and ask them to forgive you for being bitter towards them.

The process goes like this: In prayer, while praying out loud if you are able, from your heart you need to forgive the person. And this may not be easy to do. Then after you have forgiven them, you must contact them and ask for forgiveness. Again, this still is not to restore a relationship.

The Sunday evening that I preached on bitterness, there was a man there who was battling bitterness due to an ugly divorce. (I suppose there are not any pretty divorces.) He told me on Monday that yesterday, after the service Sunday evening he had to call his ex-wife in regards to where to meet to transfer their daughter back to her after the weekend. Father had her for the weekend.

He told me that her phone conversation was the usual short and coarse statements, but after the arrangements had been settled he then said to her that he had one more thing that he would like to talk to her about. With her voice sounding impatient and agitated she responded, "What?" He then told me that he said to her, *"Would you please forgive me? I have been bitter in my heart towards you and I know that it is not right. Would you please forgive me?"* He said that there was a pause of silence for a bit on the phone. When she spoke her voice was a bit gentler as she said, *"Yes, I forgive you."* He thanked her and said, *"Good-bye."*

He told me during the years that had passed since the divorce, he had done everything that I had said to do except one thing, which was to contact the person and ask for forgiveness. There lying on the couch in his living room he said tears of joy began to flow. He sensed a joy and peace flood his soul knowing that he now had the issue resolved.

How do you know if you have bitterness in your heart towards someone? One of the ways is your thought life towards that person. If you are bitter, usually when you are alone, or pillow your head at night, then you will have thoughts of vengeance. Out of the heart proceed evil thoughts.

What happened to you may have occurred many, many years earlier, yet the vengeful thoughts are as if it was yesterday. Not only that, but you will enjoy the thoughts and embellish them. All the while that old wound deep down in your heart, you're massaging it and working it so that it oozes out the poisonous thoughts. But the Holy Spirit grieves over what is happening in your spirit.

Another time out West, after I had preached on bitterness, I had a man come to me and ask me to pray for him. He told me that he had bitterness in his heart towards his boss, and at times he would have thoughts of stringing his boss up in a tree and then slicing his flesh off of his body slowly, so as to hear him scream.

Who was that? A good Christian man who was saved, married, Bible reading, praying, and serving in a church. And God showed him that there was something in his heart that was grieving the Holy Spirit, and that he needed to deal with it.

There was a time in my life where I had bitterness in my heart. I had bitterness towards my mother. Now, I did not have a bad mother at all. There was no God or religion in our home, but even so, I did not have a bad mother, nor did I have a bad home.

There was one thing though that was obvious, which was that I was the black sheep of the kids. This fostered bitterness in my heart. Even though I was now saved, and had been saved for many years, as well as preaching the word of God, yet there was bitterness in my heart that I did not realize was there. I, too, would allow my mind when I would pillow my head at night, to go down memory lane and then embellish the memories in ways that I would be ashamed to write. Thank God they are now under the blood of Jesus Christ!

I heard a sermon on bitterness and realized that I was guilty and needed to repent. By the Holy Spirit dealing with me through the sermon, I realized that I was grieving the Holy Spirit when I thought those thoughts and harbored bitterness in my heart.

My first step was to get alone with my Lord Jesus Christ in prayer and confess my sin to Him. Then I stayed on my knees until I had truly forgiven my mother. And this was not easy. My flesh wanted to continue in my sin. My flesh wanted to feel sorry for itself. It wanted to stroke itself and wallow in its self pity. My flesh, my old man, didn't want to move on. It wanted to stay there because it was at the center of all of the vengeful thoughts. In my mind I knew now that it was not right, and I had to crucify my flesh, my old man which the Bible states is corrupt.

So I stayed there in prayer until I could honestly thank God for my mother. I am ashamed to write this as I want to stress again that I did not have a bad mother. After all, she had to deal with me which at times was more than she could take. But I thought of her and how her father, my grandfather was an atheist, and I thought of how she was just lost in sin. *"Oh God,"* I prayed, *"I have been so wicked! Thank you for my mother and how good you have been to me."* I prayed on and on and joy began to fill my heart. Light and warmth flooded in where before it had been cold and hard in my heart.

After praying and getting things right in my heart, I then sat down and wrote her a letter asking her to forgive me for being bitter towards her. I told her that I was wrong and then asked her if she would forgive me. She did write me back and our relationship has been much better since, which is like whipped cream on the ice cream. But do you know what happened to me after I wrote her and asked for forgiveness? It really surprised me, too. That night, and every night since then, when I pillow my head I have not had vengeful thoughts towards her or my family. Those wicked, bitter, poisonous thoughts are gone. The root of bitterness had been pulled out.

So let's go over this as a brief review.

You have been trespassed against and it has hurt you. Bad, that you didn't deserve, came you way. Or good, that you did deserve, did not come your way, and it hurt you. Yes, it does hurt! And since the temptation is to become bitter, you may now be bitter. Your bitterness is sin and grieves the Holy Spirit of God. You need to get the victory over your bitterness.

You must go to the Lord Jesus Christ in prayer and confess to Him that you are angry, mad and bitter about what has happened to you. The Bible says, "Casting all you care upon him; for he careth for you." 1 Pet. 5:7 You don't need to beat around the bush, you need to be honest with your Lord and speak very plainly to him. He knows it anyway. What are you going to hide from him? Nothing, no matter how hard you try.

After praying and getting everything off your chest, so to speak, then the best way you know how, in prayer, you must choose to forgive that person, or whatever the circumstance was that happened to you. Wrestle it out in prayer, but let God win.

Forgiveness is a choice and it is time for you to choose to forgive and move on with your life. You have spun your wheels long enough, and you have grieved your Saviour for too long. It is time to mortify your flesh, even though it rises up and wants you to wallow in self pity. It is time, and it is God's will for you to move on with your life.

Once you have gained the victory in prayer the best way you know how, you have forgiven them.

Perhaps you have forgiven God because you were bitter towards Him. One of the main reasons God's children quit on Him is because they get mad at Him. Then the anger turns to bitterness because they know He could have prevented what happened to them, and He didn't.

Now you must contact the person, if you are able, and ask them to forgive you for being bitter towards them. This is essential in order for you to get the victory as well as to get your heart right with God. It is not designed to restore a relationship, it is so that you can get the victory and be right with God.

I don't know how to stress to you just how important this one step is. Unforgiveness is what preserves the flow of the bitter water in your soul, and that bitter water is killing, or already has killed you spiritually, and eventually physically as well.

I mentioned earlier that your bitter waters could be made sweet. To have nothing between your soul and the Saviour makes all of life sweet, and the overcoming of bitterness brings a person close to their Saviour. But there is something else to see that can make your bitter waters sweet. You need to see the hand of God in what happened to you.

The Bible says, "And we know that all things work together for good to them that love God, to them who are the called according to *his* purpose." (Rom. 8:28) If you are saved and love the

Lord, then you are called according to His purpose. (Rev. 17:14) Even the things that happened to you before you were saved, God is able to work *everything* together in your life for good. It didn't say that everything was good, but that we know all things *work together* for good.

Whatever has happened, though it may have left a very bitter taste in your mouth, yet you need to see the hand of God in it. Maybe what happened to you was not from the Lord. It might have been wicked in origin, but the Lord is still able to work it together for good.

What is amazing to me is that over the years I have seen the Lord Jesus Christ take my mistakes and weave them together in my life, in such a way, as to make it look like they should have been there all along. I have seen the Lord do that for others as well.

One of the greatest Bible examples is the life of the apostle Paul. When he went down to Jerusalem he was warned not to go and he went anyway. As a matter of fact, when he arrived in the temple at Jerusalem, God put him into a trance and told him directly to get out of town and that they would not receive his testimony. And Paul argues with the Lord about it, disobeys the Lord and ends up in prison.

I find this absolutely amazing that Paul was so set on witnessing to the Jews in Jerusalem that he argues with the Lord about it.

Acts 22:17 And it came to pass, that,

> when I was come again to Jerusalem, even while I prayed in the temple, I was in a trance;
>
> Acts 22:18 And saw him saying unto me, Make haste, and get thee quickly out of Jerusalem: for they will not receive thy testimony concerning me.
>
> Acts 22:19 And I said, Lord, they know that I imprisoned and beat in every synagogue them that believed on thee:
>
> Acts 22:20 And when the blood of thy martyr Stephen was shed, I also was standing by, and consenting unto his death, and kept the raiment of them that slew him.
>
> Acts 22:21 And he said unto me, Depart: for I will send thee far hence unto the Gentiles.

The Lord then takes Paul and uses him even while he is in prison in such a way as to make it look like that's how it was supposed to be.

You may ask, *"Well, wasn't that how it was supposed to be? After all, some of the Bible was written by Paul when he was in prison."* All I can say is that I am no Calvinist, but God worked it all together for good.

Stop and think about this. You might be going to Heaven because of what happened to you. There has been many a person who was a black sheep, sick, rejected by loved ones, poor, or betrayed by friends and because of what they have gone through it prepared them to hear the gospel.

Then someone came along, or they may have found a tract, or turned to Billy Graham on YouTube. And when they heard how Jesus Christ loved them and paid the price for their sins on the Cross, they accepted Jesus Christ as their personal Saviour and were born again. If the bitter trials that they had gone through had not happened, then they would never have wanted to get saved and would have ended up going to Hell.

The following story was told to me by the lady herself.

Years ago in the Midwest there was a man with a family. He was the largest corn farmer in the United States. Sadly though, his wife died. In the process of time he met another lady and they soon married, but she did not care for his daughter, whom I will call Sally. (Sally was the one who told me this story.) Sally's stepmother had her own children and favored them. Her father was not strong enough to stand up to his new wife, so Sally became the black sheep with constant rejection in the family. They were a strong Roman Catholic family.

In time her father ended up dying as well, and as you can imagine there was quite a bit of wealth associated with such a large operation. But Sally's stepmother had legal documents arranged to where Sally got nothing from her father's estate. It all went to her stepmother and her children.

Sally, who was now in her seventies, told me that there was one newspaper clipping on the wall by the refrigerator that was always special to her as it was an article about her father written in the local paper. Though it had no monetary value, yet when she asked for it, they snapped at her and said, *"No!"* She was to get nothing.

Then as she looked at me she said, in her gentle, peaceful voice, and I shall never forget it. *"If I had not had all that happen to me, then I never would have gotten saved. I am the one who is truly rich. And now I go visit them at holidays and I witness to them. They hate me and don't want me around, but I love them and tell them about Jesus."*

There is a lady whose bitter waters have been made sweet because she saw the hand of God in the bitter trial. Her bitter waters have been made oh so sweet for they moved her to drink of the water of life, freely.

At the risk of being tedious I am going to write one more story of how to get victory over your bitterness. The following true story illustrates the steps that I have tried to convey in this chapter. And I want to stress again, this is so very important for you to gain the victory in your heart and life.

One Sunday morning a preacher, whom I will name Pastor Smith, was preaching on the subject of getting victory over bitterness. In the sermon he mentioned that if you have bitterness in your heart towards someone that you needed to forgive them. You then needed to contact them and ask for forgiveness for being bitter towards them. This was necessary in order to get the victory over your bitterness.

After the sermon seven ladies together came up to him. Each one told him how she had been molested by a stepfather. Then they all looked at him with astonishment and said, *"We have to go ask him for forgiveness?"*

Pastor Smith then told them, *"This is not to restore a relationship or to create one. This is so you can gain the victory over your bitterness."*

They understood, went home and in prayer each one on her own, the best way she knew how, forgave the stepfather that had molested her. Then they each tried to contact the man and in so doing ask him for forgiveness.

That Sunday evening, the service was just getting started as they began to sing some hymns of worship. After the first hymn was sung, excitedly these ladies asked if they could give a testimony about what had happened that afternoon, to which Pastor Smith was more than eager to allow.

One by one each of the ladies gave a testimony of how for the first time in many years she no longer had bitterness in her heart towards her stepfather. One lady stood and told of how she had called her stepfather and asked him to forgive her for being bitter towards him. She said that her stepfather began to cry, and as he cried he said, *"You're asking me to forgive you? I am the one that should be asking you to forgive me."* A couple of the other ladies gave a very similar testimony.

There were others who said that the man was

now dead and they were not able to talk to him, to which Pastor Smith told them that they would just have to go to God and get it settled with him then. But each one of those ladies gave the testimony that for the first time in many years they no longer had anger and bitterness in their heart towards the man that had molested them.

Their lives had a new joy, a new freedom, a new sweetness. What's more is that they could now move on with their lives.

Were they reconciled to those men? No! But they were now much closer to the Lord Jesus Christ.

Chapter 3

Rebuke

Eph. 4:31 Let all bitterness, and wrath, and anger, and clamour, and evil speaking, be put away from you, with all malice
32 And be ye kind one to another, tenderhearted, forgiving one another, even as God for Christ's sake hath forgiven you.

"...even as God."

So God is our example of how to forgive, and you will notice that in these verses it says, "One to another" and, "One another." That makes the context of forgiveness here "*horizontal*" or another way to put it is between each other.

There is a procedure that God sets forth in order for people to be reconciled to Him. That procedure is the same way you and I are to deal with the trespasses and divisions that happen in our lives. That's why it says, "...even as God." The way God forgives us is the way we are to forgive others. As we have already covered, there are such things as trespasses that occur between us and others, between others and us.

God will rebuke you, but He is always right and never trespasses against you. "Shall not the Judge of all the earth do right?" (Gen. 18:25) He may lead you into situations that you do not desire, or He may call you to fields that you fear to go to, but He never trespasses against you. You see, the Lord Jesus Christ owns you, if you are saved, and He bought you with His blood that He shed on Calvary. He is the best Master and always treats you better than you deserve.

Perhaps you ask, how I can make that statement? I can make that statement easily because if I, or you, got what we deserved, we would be in the fires of Hell weeping, wailing and gnashing our teeth. From there we would stand before God at the White Throne Judgment and see that our name does not appear in the Book of Life. Then we would bow the knee and confess that Jesus is Lord right before He casts us into the Lake of Fire. "And whosoever was not found written in the book of life was cast into the lake of fire." (Rev. 20:15) That's why I can easily say that He never treats me wrong nor trespasses against me.

Not only that, is the fact the He loves us more

than we can ever imagine and only desires what is *right* for us. He knows what is *right*, but we must remember He is looking at it from an eternal standpoint and not from a temporal physical standpoint. Often we will view life from our physical standpoint which means we are viewing it in light of comfort for our flesh. God does not view it that way. What is right for us is sometimes painful.

In life, before God and before man, trespasses take place. There is no doubt about that. Those trespasses break the unity or fellowship that the two parties once enjoyed. Where once there was togetherness, joy, delight and love; now, after the trespass there is a wound, hurt, sorrow, and often times anger. So if God is our example, now that the trespass has occurred, what does He do?

Let's start at the very beginning of a life. Let's start with a little child. When that child is born he (or she) is innocent. He has no knowledge of right and wrong, therefore if a little child dies, he (or she) goes to Heaven. Notice what the word of God says,

> 2Sam. 12:22 And he said, While the child was yet alive, I fasted and wept: for I said, Who can tell *whether* GOD will be gracious to me, that the child may live?
>
> 2Sam. 12:23 But now he is dead, wherefore should I fast? can I bring him back again? I shall go to him, but he shall not return to me.

But as the child grows older there is a point where it comes to the age of accountability. That is the age when the child understands right and wrong. There is no set age for this point in someone's life. It varies from person to person, home to home and nation to nation. Some people never reach the age of accountability, such as retarded feeble minded people.

A child that is raised around the word of God is going to have the knowledge of good and evil, of right and wrong, much earlier than a child who is raised around evolution and atheism. The knowledge of right and wrong is an individual thing between that person and the Lord Jesus Christ.

Some have said it is the time when a person becomes ashamed if they are naked. A little child is not ashamed when they are naked, but there comes a time when they are. I don't know if I could say that Is it or not.

A pastor that I know had each of his children come to him as they grew older and tell him that they wanted to get saved. When each did that he would say to them, *"You do? Why do you want to get saved?"* Of course, they were around preaching and the word of God constantly. They would reply to him, *"Because I don't want to go to Hell."* He then would ask them, *"Are you a sinner?"* Usually they would say no to this question. Then he would tell them, *"Well, you have nothing to worry about because only sinners go to Hell. But don't sin because if you sin then you are going to go to Hell."*

He would let them go, and then he would pray for them that God would give them understanding of sin and judgement. He told me that after a week or two they would get a very serious look on their face and not long after that they would come to him and say, *"Daddy, I want to get saved."* He would again ask them, *"Are you a sinner?"* This time they would nervously reply, *"Yes, I am a sinner."* He would then pray with them and lead them to the Lord Jesus Christ.

What happened is that the Holy Spirit rebuked them in their heart, and they knew the Lord Jesus Christ was not happy with them. This is the first step in the process of reconciliation between God and and individual. Even as God lets the offending party know what they have done wrong, that is our example of how we are to proceed in the process of person to person reconciliation.

I must qualify this though, because your salvation is not a process, and the actual act of reconciliation in regards to salvation is not a long-term process. It is a new birth that happens in a single moment of time, not over a long period of time.

But for a person who is already saved, when they trespass against the Lord the fellowship is immediately broken. God immediately becomes distant from you. The fellowship is broken, and the Holy Spirit is quenched.

Gal. 5:19 Now the works of the flesh are

manifest, which are *these*; Adultery,
fornication, uncleanness, lasciviousness,
20 Idolatry, witchcraft, hatred, variance,
emulations, wrath, strife, seditions,
heresies,
21 Envyings, murders, drunkenness,
revellings, and such like: of the which I
tell you before, as I have also told *you* in
time past, that they which do such things
shall not inherit the kingdom of God.

Lest you should fear the verse, notice that it says *"inherit"* the kingdom of God. This is not a reference to your salvation. It is a reference to your inheritance which is given out at the Millenium in the form of reigning over cities with Jesus Christ. (Luke 19, Rom. 8, 2 Tim. 2:12, Rev. 20) But it does show that there are actions in the flesh by saved Christians that grieve and quench the Lord in your walk and life. Not only do you lose fellowship with Him now, but if you don't judge yourself now you will suffer loss of rewards later.

Using God as our example then, the first thing that He does when He has been trespassed against is to rebuke the offending party. This is the same thing that happened before you got saved. God let you know that you were lost and on your way to Hell. He let you know that He was not pleased with you.

One of the ways He did this was to give the Light to every one when they are born. "*That* was the true Light, which lighteth every man that cometh into the world." (John 1:9) Every one is born with the knowledge that there is a God. Man has to be educated out of his knowledge that there is a God. You don't find atheists in the jungles, you find them in the universities. Man is born with a knowledge of God.

This knowledge bears witness in man when he grows older that something is not right between him and God. He doesn't know who God is, but He knows something is not right.

> Rom. 2:14 "For when the Gentiles, which have not the law, do by nature the things contained in the law, these, having not the law, are a law unto themselves:
> 15 Which shew the work of the law written in their hearts, their conscience also bearing witness, and *their* thoughts the mean while accusing or else excusing one another.
> Rom. 1:20 For the invisible things of him from the creation of the world are clearly seen, being understood by the things that are made, *even* his eternal power and Godhead; so that they are without excuse.

The best thing that can happen to you is for God to contact you and rebuke you; yet man most often runs from the rebuke of God. "Because strait *is* the gate, and narrow *is* the way, which leadeth unto life, and few there be that find it." (Matt. 7:14)

I am a preacher and my call is to "Preach the word; be instant in season, out of season; reprove, rebuke, exhort with all longsuffering and doctrine." (2 Tim. 4:2) Two-thirds of the call to preach is negative. It is to reprove and to rebuke.

There is less and less of this type of preaching taking place in the world today. Most of the saved will not endure being rebuked, but if you want to have a close walk with your Saviour then in the Laodicean period, which is what we are now in, then you are to be ready and able to receive a rebuke.

> As many as I love, I rebuke and chasten: be zealous therefore, and repent. (Rev. 3:19)
>
> For the commandment *is* a lamp; and the law *is* light; and reproofs of instruction *are* the way of life. (Prov. 6:23)

It is sad, but in these last days right before the Rapture, most of God's people are more concerned about how they *"feel"* than whether or not their Lord Jesus Christ is offended. The same is true between each other as well.

I can understand Satan attempting to stop the rebuke of God because he wants to see as many souls in Hell as he can, but man in his fallen condition runs from, rejects, and rebels against the rebuke of God.

I am a preacher and God has called me to preach. As one who is called to preach, I must say that it is hard to get up in the pulpit night after night, week after week, and reprove, rebuke, and exhort. Why? People do not like you when you do that. They don't want to be rebuked, they want to feel good about themselves.

It is such a difficult task that the vast majority of modern preachers have studied how to preach so as to avoid all rebuking and reproving. They have studied how to be positive and encouraging, so as to bring about a better you. They are not doing their job!

The job of an auto mechanic is to find out what is wrong with your car and fix it. The job of a doctor (not this holistic, fake witchcraft, but a true doctor) is to find out what is wrong with you and fix it. And the job of a preacher is to find out what is wrong and preach against it, while at the same time giving the solution to the problem from the word of God.

You must admit though, that to the world it does look kind of strange. The world watches people go into a church building and give money to get yelled at for an hour. You know that looks weird to the world, but it is the way the Lord has chosen to operate in this age. In the Old Testament he sent prophets. In the New Testament he sends preachers, and the preachers that He sends are common people.

> 26 For ye see your calling, brethren, how that not many wise men after the flesh, not many mighty, not many noble, *are called*:
>
> 27 But God hath chosen the foolish things of the world to confound the wise; and God hath chosen the weak things of the world to confound the things which are mighty. (1Cor. 1:26-27)

Not very many of God called-preachers are doctors and lawyers. The vast majority of true God-called preachers are common men. They are not polished, fancy, and many are not very educated in relation to the world. I have preached for many a man who has never graduated from high school, and who has never even gone to a Bible school or Christian college to learn how to preach. God just called him and put him right into the ministry. "Cry aloud, spare not, lift up thy voice like a trumpet, and shew my people their transgression, and the house of Jacob their sins." (Is. 58:1)

Do you know what is hard about "shewing" God's people their sins? They start looking at your sins in order to justify their sins. Ah yes, that old Adamic nature of man. One day we will shed it for a glorified, new, sinless, perfect body, praise the Lord!

King David had committed adultery with Bathsheba, and she got pregnant. He then called her husband Uriah, who was out fighting a war with the army of Israel, back to Jerusalem. King David then got Uriah drunk, in hopes that he would go home and lie with his wife, Bathsheba, but Uriah wouldn't do it. David then sends him back to the battle with orders for him to be killed in the battle. Once Uriah is killed, then David marries Bathsheba, trying to cover up the adultery. There is one big problem though. What are you going to hide from God?

One day God sends a prophet to David by the name of Nathan. God gives Nathan a message to deliver to David, "Thou art the man!" God rebukes David. David had sinned against God and God rebukes him.

With God as our example then, the first step is to rebuke the one who has trespassed against us. "If thy brother trespass against thee, rebuke him..." (Luke 17:3) That is what the word of God says you are supposed to do. You are to go to the person and rebuke them and tell them that what they did was wrong. This is not easy to do!

I heard Dr. Bob Jones Sr. on the radio one day. It was an audio recording of when he was talking to a class of student preachers. He was covering:

> Luke 17:3 "Take heed to yourselves: If thy brother trespass against thee, rebuke him; and if he repent, forgive him.
>
> 4 And if he trespass against thee seven times in a day, and seven times in a day turn again to thee, saying, I repent; thou shalt forgive him.

One of the points he made was that, it is not easy to be a Christian, especially if you are going to obey those two verses, and he was right.

If someone has trespassed against you then it is your duty, according to the Scriptures, to go to them and rebuke them. That is not easy to do. This is why I stated in the last chapter that to forgive them between you and the Lord, vertically, is so important. It's like taking this giant step of going to them and rebuking them and making two smaller steps out of the one large step.

By already forgiving them, the anger is gone. The hurt and pain are gone. Anger, hurt and pain are like roadblocks that prevent you from moving on to victory. With those emotions out of the way the step of rebuking them is much easier to take. It is not *easy*, but *easier* to take.

And if you were bitter, then for your personal victory you are going to be contacting them anyway. The very act of your contacting them and rehersing the incident to them, and thus asking for forgiveness will usually be sufficient enough to act as a rebuke. But some people are a bit slow and you can include a statement as you ask for forgiveness for being bitter towards them that what they had done was not right. Having already forgiven them really does make this step of going to the person and rebuking them a little easier.

You are the one that has been trespassed against so why should you go to the person other than it is commanded in the scriptures? Because they may not know that they have offended you. If you assume that they do, you might be wrong.

Perhaps you say that they *ought* to know that what they did was wrong. Maybe they ought to, but it is possible that they do not know, so you have to go to them and rebuke them. This way you will now know that they know what they did to you was wrong.

If you do not go to them, then there is a good chance that you are going to end up bitter, if you are not already, over the whole thing. Why? Because if you are around them, you are going to have to act like everything is alright, when if the truth were known everything is not alright. You become a hypocrite. You are acting one way, and it is the opposite of the way you really are. It is not how you truly feel.

God will not act like all is well when it is not well. God rebukes the trespasser, and so must you. "Open rebuke *is* better than secret love." (Prov. 27:5)

Have you been hurt? Have you had someone trespass against you? Then you need to let them know, and you need to rebuke them. God uses the spoken word through people and preachers, but God also uses His written word. As a matter of fact, the written word is His primary way He rebukes people.

I mention that because you can go to them in person, or you can write them a letter, but either way you must let them know what they did wrong and how they trespassed against you.

In Genesis 3 God comes looking for Adam after Adam and Eve have partaken of the Tree of the Knowledge of Good and Evil. He calls to Adam, "Where *art* thou?" Did God know where Adam was? Of course He did! Why did He call then? Because He was making Adam aware of where Adam was. He was gently rebuking Adam and Eve, but letting them know that they had done wrong and that He was not pleased with them. What they had done, by partaking of the Tree of the Knowledge of Good and Evil, was that they had disobeyed God and thus they had trespassed against God. God rebuked them for it.

There is a king in the Bible by the name of Ahab, and next door to his palace was a vineyard which was owned by Naboth. Ahab coveted that vineyard, but Naboth would not sell it to king Ahab because it was forbidden under the law of Moses to be sold. The land was, commanded by God in the law, to remain in the family as an inheritance. Because of this Naboth would not sell it. Naboth was doing right. Ahab's wife, Jezebel, has Naboth killed, and then tells Ahab to take possession of Naboth's vineyard so he could plant his garden of herbs. But God sends a prophet by the name of Elijah to rebuke Ahab for what he had done.

> 1Kings 21:17 And the word of the LORD came to Elijah the Tishbite, saying,
> 18 Arise, go down to meet Ahab king of Israel, which *is* in Samaria: behold, *he is* in

the vineyard of Naboth, whither he is
gone down to possess it.
19 And thou shalt speak unto him,
saying, Thus saith the LORD, Hast thou
killed, and also taken possession? And
thou shalt speak unto him, saying, Thus
saith the LORD, In the place where dogs
licked the blood of Naboth shall dogs lick
thy blood, even thine.
20 And Ahab said to Elijah, Hast thou
found me, O mine enemy? And he
answered, I have found *thee*: because thou
hast sold thyself to work evil in the sight
of the LORD.
21 Behold, I will bring evil upon thee,
and will take away thy posterity, and will
cut off from Ahab him that pisseth against
the wall, and him that is shut up and left
in Israel,
22 And will make thine house like the
house of Jeroboam the son of Nebat, and
like the house of Baasha the son of
Ahijah, for the provocation wherewith
thou hast provoked *me* to anger, and made
Israel to sin.
23 And of Jezebel also spake the LORD,
saying, The dogs shall eat Jezebel by the
wall of Jezreel.
24 Him that dieth of Ahab in the city the
dogs shall eat; and him that dieth in the
field shall the fowls of the air eat.

God is very angry and thus gives Ahab quite a rebuke through Elijah! But there is something that happens after Ahab receives this rebuke from the Lord, and that is, Ahab repents.

> 1Kings 21:27 And it came to pass, when Ahab heard those words, that he rent his clothes, and put sackcloth upon his flesh, and fasted, and lay in sackcloth, and went softly.
> 28 And the word of the LORD came to Elijah the Tishbite, saying,
> 29 Seest thou how Ahab humbleth himself before me? because he humbleth himself before me, I will not bring the evil in his days: *but* in his son's days will I bring the evil upon his house.

The proper action that is to take place after a legitimate rebuke is given, is for the person to repent. This is what Ahab does, he repents of what he has done, and God lets him know that the judgement will be delayed until after Ahab is dead.

Have you ever been rebuked? In this age all you have to do is raise your voice, and people think that you are rebuking them. Being yelled at is not always a rebuke. If you are working a job and the boss yells at you to hurry up, get to work, or to let you know that he wants you to start working on something else, that is not a rebuke.

A rebuke is to let you know what you are doing wrong, or what you have done wrong. The purpose is to let you know that you are in the wrong so that you will repent of what you have done. "If thy brother trespass against thee, rebuke him; and if he repent, forgive him." (Luke 17:3)

When I was in Bible school another man there who had hurt his back and was in pain. This man had asked me for a ride from California to Florida when I left home for Bible school. I had told him that I would give him a ride, and then I changed my mind, but I changed my mind after he was counting on me to give him a ride.

At school, after he hurt his back, I told him that I would bring him a heating pad that night for his back. That night in the evening service he asked me for the heating pad, and I forgot to bring it. A few days later he came up to me and sharply rebuked me for the two incidents of where I had not kept my word and had let him down.

It was like a sharp knife pierced my soul, as I knew he was right and I was wrong. A few days after, I found him and apologized to him for my failures concerning him. Even as I write this story it still bothers me. I am thankful that he forgave me.

Can you take a rebuke? There are many who cannot. Some people have the hardest time admitting they are wrong. That is not good. You may end up in Hell because of it, for in order to get saved you must accept God's rebuke that you have broken His law and are guilty. You must admit that you are wrong and have done wrong. If you cannot do this, you will end up in Hell.

Is there someone that you need to go to and rebuke? Are you carrying around emotions and animosity about someone, but you have not gone to them and rebuked them for what they did? According to the word of God, you are commanded to go to them and rebuke them. It doesn't matter if it is family or friend, you are to go to them.

Perhaps you have a fear that they will get mad, or that it won't do any good. You cannot let your assumptions and fears stop you from doing what God has told you to do. The responsibility is on you according to the word of God. But if you are right and they do not repent, then comes division, but you must accept the fact that the division may be the direct will of God. Actually the division is already there. After the rebuke, it became manifested.

I know that may sound strange to say that it might be the direct will of God, but to bring division is one of the reasons Jesus came according to Luke 12:51-53. I quoted and commented on these verses in the previous chapter Transgressed, but there is more that needs to be written about these verses.

> Luke 12:51 Suppose ye that I am come to give peace on earth? I tell you, Nay; but rather division:
>
> 52 For from henceforth there shall be five in one house divided, three against two, and two against three.
>
> 53 The father shall be divided against

> the son, and the son against the father; the mother against the daughter, and the daughter against the mother; the mother in law against her daughter in law, and the daughter in law against her mother in law.

Does a family member of yours need to be rebuked? Have they trespassed against you and thus hurt or broken your heart? If so, then you are commanded by God to rebuke them. The temptation comes to smooth it over, to ignore it and to proceed as if it never happened. The Bible does say, "He that covereth a transgression seeketh love." (Prov. 17:9) So you may have a grace period and overlook the transgression. The Lord is very patient with us, and we should have grace one with another. But depending on the severity of the transgression, or the attitude of the individual, or if the transgression is being repeated, there will come a point where a rebuke is due and commanded by God.

> 1Sam. 2:12 Now the sons of Eli *were* sons of Belial; they knew not the LORD.
>
> 17 Wherefore the sin of the young men was very great before the Lord: for men abhorred the offering of the LORD.
>
> 22 Now Eli was very old, and heard all that his sons did unto all Israel; and how they lay with the women that assembled at the door of the tabernacle of the congregation.

> 1Sam. 3:13 For I (The LORD) have told him (Eli) that I will judge his house for ever for the iniquity which he knoweth; because his sons made themselves vile, and he restrained them not.

So both of Eli's sons die in one day and it was the same day that Eli heard the news that the Ark was taken by the Philistines Eli fell off a bench backwards and broke his neck and died.

I have a question for you. Who do you love more, the Lord Jesus Christ, or your friends and loved ones? Is Jesus Christ first, or is family first? If you are having trouble with friends or family could it be that the Lord is testing you to see who you love more? Sadly in this age many have put friends and family before the Lord Jesus Christ.

Hey Momma! There comes a time in such cases when it is sin to keep the peace. The statement, *"But it's family"* no longer applies. The statement that applies now is, *"But it's the Lord Jesus Christ and the word of God."* Is your family an idol? It was to Eli, and God brought judgement upon him and his sons, all in one day.

There are many many stories, along the lines of this one that I am going to write, but this one will illustrate the truth.

Years ago in a small town God touched the heart of a young man and called him to preach. In pursuit of his call he began to study the Bible and to take classes on preaching and the ministry.

From time to time opportunity would arise for him to preach in his church, on the streets, in jails and nursing homes. And he was very good at preaching; the power of God was present when he proclaimed the word of God.

He got married and had some children. As his children grew, they began to dabble in sin and live very loosely, even though they were still living at home. He tried to correct them, but his wife would step in between him and the kids. Momma would side against him. Try as he would, he was challenged by his entire family.

Over time his zeal for preaching grew cold. His children got into sin deeper and deeper, until eventually that man no longer even believed he was called to preach. Because of family opposition, and in order to keep the peace, he backed down and put Jesus Christ second to his family. His kids ended up in sodomy, drugs and rebellion, even while still living at home. Even with such wickedness, he would not deal with it. He turned his back on the Lord Jesus Christ. That is what Eli did, and he ended up dead from the judgement of God.

You are either going to put Jesus Christ first, or you will have to sin against Him, and He is going to put you in that position on purpose.

Today many families are broken. Divorce has wrought havoc on the young people of our day. And if you are a parent who is trying to live and do right then you know the likely result if you rebuke your kids and put your foot down. You are going to lose them, and possibly even lose any sort of visitation. What are you going to do? I'm not trying to be hard, but you must do right and put Jesus Christ first. The smile of your Saviour ought to be more important to you than the smile of your children, your family or your friends. "Suppose ye that I am come to give peace on earth? I tell you, Nay; but rather division." (Luke 12:51)

Why did the Lord come to bring division? And the division in the context is family. The Lord wants to know if He is first. Usually family is who you love the most. Is Jesus Christ first in your heart? Do your actions show it? Is it time for you to rebuke someone? Perhaps you have smoothed it over long enough. Right is right, and the Lord Jesus Christ must come first.

Chapter 4
Repent

Eph. 4:32 Even as God...

Luke 17:3 Take heed to yourselves: If thy brother trespass against thee, rebuke him; and if he repent, forgive him.

Luke 17:4 And if he trespass against thee seven times in a day, and seven times in a day turn again to thee, saying, I repent; thou shalt forgive him.

How did God forgive me? What was it that caused God to forgive me?

The first thing that I had to realize is that I had transgressed His commandments. I was guilty before God. This fact was borne witness to within my bosom by the, "...true Light, which lighteth every man that cometh into the world." (John 1:9)

Along with this internal witness, God sent a person, or the word of God to rebuke me and let me know that I was not right with Him. He rebuked me by telling me that He was angry with me and if I didn't *repent* and turn to the Lord Jesus Christ for my salvation, that I was going to go to Hell when I died.

In this age, repentance is a doctrine that is not mentioned much. In regards to salvation, some preach if you require repentance as part of salvation then you are adding to the gospel. Specifically the claim is that you are adding works to salvation. While there is no doubt that salvation is by grace through faith, yet proper repentance is needed for real salvation.

William Booth, the founder of the Salvation Army, when the Army was a militant force for the Kingdom of God, said, *"...I consider that the chief dangers which confront the coming century will be religion without the Holy Ghost, Christianity without Christ, forgiveness without repentance, salvation without regeneration, politics without God, and Heaven without Hell."*

Repentance is necessary in order to be saved.

> 3 I tell you, Nay: but, except ye repent, ye shall all likewise perish. (Luke 13:3)
>
> 7 I say unto you, that likewise joy shall be in heaven over one sinner that repenteth, more than over ninety and nine just persons, which need no repentance. (Luke 15:7)

Before you were saved, there was a time when you *thought* that you were good. You *thought* that between you and God everything was fine, after all you hadn't killed anyone. But in order for you to get saved, you had to get to the place where you realized that you were not good, that you were not alright before God. As a matter of fact, you realized that God was very angry with you. Maybe it was not mentioned that God was very angry with you, but you knew enough to realize that you were not going to make it to Heaven the way you were. You had a change of mind about yourself; that is repentance.

I have heard the accusation that stressing repentance is the same as adding works to salvation, but this is not true. For repentance is a change of mind. Works ought to follow the change of mind but are not *required* by Scripture, for then you would be adding works to salvation.

Works ought to follow repentance. But just like the dying thief asked Jesus Christ to remember him when he came into His kingdom, so too, works are not always evident. If your mind is changed, then it is likely that your actions will change as well to match your repentance, but sometimes it takes a while for the change to be made manifest.

There is the possibility as well to have a change in works without repentance. Many a person has started going to church, turned over a "new leaf," and made amends to their life, but on the inside they are no different, for they have never repented on the inside. They are no different in their heart and thus still on their way to Hell.

Consider the following story in the word of God. What I am about to show you, in my opinion is absolutely amazing.

The Bible is different from all other religious books on the face of the earth. There is no other religious book on earth that claims to show man what to do in order to achieve Heaven, Nirvana, Paradise or any other description of positive eternal existence, that has a story in it like the one I am about to show you.

Here is a story about a murderer who tells God to repent. Can you imagine that? A murderer tells God to repent!

> Ex. 32:9 And the LORD said unto Moses, I have seen this people, and, behold, it *is* a stiffnecked people:
>
> 10 Now therefore let me alone, that my wrath may wax hot against them, and that I may consume them: and I will make of thee a great nation.
>
> 11 And Moses besought the LORD his God, and said, LORD, why doth thy wrath wax hot against thy people, which thou hast brought forth out of the land of Egypt with great power, and with a mighty hand?
>
> 12 Wherefore should the Egyptians

speak, and say, For mischief did he bring
them out, to slay them in the mountains,
and to consume them from the face of the
earth? Turn from thy fierce wrath, and
repent of this evil against thy people.
13 Remember Abraham, Isaac, and
Israel, thy servants, to whom thou swarest
by thine own self, and saidst unto them, I
will multiply your seed as the stars of
heaven, and all this land that I have
spoken of will I give unto your seed, and
they shall inherit *it* for ever.
14 And the LORD repented of the evil
which he thought to do unto his people.

The first thing to notice is that God tells Moses to, "Let me alone, that my wrath may wax hot against them, and that I may consume them."

Imagine that! God tells Moses to leave Him alone so He can get mad at them to destroy them. Who said that? JEHOVAH God said that! There is not another book on the face of the earth that portrays its God like that.

God says, *"Moses, leave me alone so that my wrath can get hot against them and I will destroy them. Then I will make a great nation out of thee."* God is getting ready to destroy Israel. They are under the wrath of God at this point, just like in John 3:36, "He that believeth not the Son shall not see life; but the wrath of God abideth on him." That is the condition that you and I were in before we got saved.

But Moses, a murderer, intercedes for God's people Israel. Why do I claim he is a murderer?

> Ex. 2:11 And it came to pass in those days, when Moses was grown, that he went out unto his brethren, and looked on their burdens: and he spied an Egyptian smiting an Hebrew, one of his brethren.
> 12 And he looked this way and that way, and when he saw that *there was* no man, he slew the Egyptian, and hid him in the sand.

Here is a murderer persuading Almighty God to not do what He is getting ready to do. I find this absolutely amazing!

The first thing Moses says is, *"Lord, those are your people that you brought out of Egypt."* Two verses earlier God tells Moses that those are his people, Ex. 32:7 And the LORD said unto Moses, Go, get thee down; for thy people, which thou broughtest out of the land of Egypt... Moses is quick to remind the Lord that those people are the Lord's people.

The second thing Moses says is, *"What will the Egyptians say?"* Lord, all of Egypt is watching you. They have seen what you did to them in Egypt, and do you want them to say that you brought them out just to kill them in the wilderness? Obviously the answer is no.

Then as Moses reasons with the Lord, who is getting ready to destroy His own people, he tells the Lord to repent. What? Yes that's right, a murderer tells God to repent. Moses tells God to, "...repent of this evil against thy people." (Ex. 32:12)

Now this repentance is not a repentance of sin, for God is holy. This repentance is a repentance of judgement, In the word of God there are examples of where God says, "Behold, I will bring evil upon thee." (1Kings 21:21) That reference right there is in reference to Ahab.

Elijah has just come to him and is pronouncing God's judgement against him in the first person, "I will bring evil upon thee." That is an evil of judgement, not a sinful or Satanic evil.

Here is another example, "Set up the standard toward Zion: retire, stay not: for I will bring evil from the north, and a great destruction." (Jer. 4:6) This evil has to do with the judgement of God, which is in the context of Exodus 32. God is getting ready to kill them for their blatant idolatry. So the evil has to do with God bringing judgement upon Israel, and Moses talks Him out of it. Moses tells God to turn from His fierce wrath and repent of this evil against His people, and guess what? *God repents!*

There is something else that I find absolutely astonishing about this. Israel is encamped not far from Mt. Sinai. The place where they make the altar and are dancing around the golden calf, they can plainly see Mt. Sinai. (By the way, did you know that in the late '70's, or early '80's, Ron Wyatt found that altar and climbed up on it, dug down into the cracks of it and found gold dust? "And he took the calf which they had made, and burnt *it* in the fire, and ground *it* to powder..." (Ex. 32:20)) Israel can plainly see the top of Sinai from where they are. They can plainly see the top of the mount burning with fire, yet with a clear manifestation of Almighty God right in front of their eyes, they still backslide and fall into sin.

"And the LORD repented of the evil which he thought to do unto his people." (Ex. 32:14) What happened? God changed his mind. Did you get that? God changed his mind from what he was getting ready to do.

This is the classic example of repentance because there is no sin involved. It is the mind of Almighty God changing from what He was getting ready to do and then ends up not doing it. God repented of the evil that He was getting ready to do.

The essence of repentance is a change of mind. Again I want to emphasize that God had not done wrong, nor was He getting ready to do wrong. The Bible says, "Shall not the Judge of all the earth do right?" (Gen. 18:25) But that cannot be said of you. You have done wrong and you are getting ready to do wrong, whether you are saved or lost. "If we say that we have no sin, we deceive ourselves, and the truth is not in us." (1 John 1:8)

Repentance is a change of mind. For you and I, repentance has to do with right and wrong. Specifically it has to do with realizing something is wrong, or a sin, when before you thought that it was alright. To claim that repentance requires works is where the problem comes in. *The works are a secondary result of the repentance, but the primary action was the change of mind.* That may be technical, but it is important in this age in which we live.

There is no doubt that God changed His mind, because Israel was not destroyed. His repentance affected his actions. If you repent, then your actions ought to be changed from that point on.

This is difficult in regards to salvation because when you got saved you ended up with a dual nature. By that I mean that you ended up, as the Bible puts it in Ephesians 4, with an old man and a new man. The old man doesn't want to do right, and the new man does, but you still have a free will as to which one you are going to obey at any given moment.

Let me give you an illustration of it. Here is a Christian sitting on a chair in the living room of his house. On his lap is his Bible open to the place where he is reading in his daily devotions. Perhaps he reads five pages a day. His Bible is open to where he needs to read for that day, yet in front of him the television is on and one of his lost brothers or sisters is watching a bad sinful movie. The music is sinful, the scenes are sinful and he knows it.

He tries to read his Bible, but then he looks up and watches some of the movie. The new man, along with the Holy Spirit, is dealing with him about the need to read his Bible, and that he should leave the room to go somewhere else where he can read his Bible without distraction. The old man is lusting for more of the movie and causing him to stay and watch just a little bit more.

Both the old man and the new man are at work. There is great internal conflict, and the deciding factor involves the Christian's free will. The amount of allowed influence from the old man is dependent on his love for Jesus Christ. You will allow sin in your life in relation to how much, or how deep your love for Jesus Christ is. And your love for Him will motivate you to read your Bible and privately pray to your Saviour. It has been said, *"Sin will keep you from the Bible, or the Bible will keep you from sin."*

When you give in to the flesh and you know that you have done wrong then it is time to confess your sins to your Saviour, Jesus Christ. Get them forgiven and removed from hindering your fellowship with Him. But in order to see the need to confess your sins you must repent of what you have done. You allowed yourself to watch and listen to what you know you should not have done. You need to repent and confess it to your Saviour.

Now in regards to someone who has rebuked you, then you must repent of what you did to them, and it was to them, for the Bible says, "If thy brother trespass against thee, rebuke him." (Luke 17:3)

If the accusation is true, will you accept it or reject it? If you are saved then there was a day when God came to you and told you that you had trespassed against Him and you are headed for Hell because you are lost. You accepted the truth about yourself, believed on the Lord Jesus Christ,were born again, and now you are on your way to Heaven. But will you accept the truth about yourself if it comes from a person? Can you take a rebuke? Can you repent after taking a rebuke? Can you change your mind about yourself, or an action that you did?

If you accept the rebuke and repent, then your actions will change. One of the first actions, if you have genuinely repented, will be to ask for forgiveness from that person. This is an act of humbling yourself and the flesh hates it!

There are times in the ministry that things are said that get taken wrong, or you mention things and it comes out wrong. A preacher is called to talk a lot, and sooner or later things are going to be said that shouldn't be said. Sometimes the Lord is just checking to see if you are full of pride or not.

Well, I was in a meeting and I said some things that got taken wrong. They were partly true, but not all of the way. It got back to the person and really troubled them. As a matter of fact they were in tears over it. When I found out, at first I couldn't even remember what I had said. Then it came to me. Though they didn't come and rebuke me, they could have rightfully done so, and if they would have I would have realized my error sooner.

Some time passed after the fact and I was returned to their church for a meeting. During the invitation I was troubled knowing that they had been hurt and that I had offended them. I went to the person and asked for forgiveness. I told them that I was sorry for what I had said and would they please forgive me? There was a short space where they seemed to hesitate, and then said some things about those who were with me. I didn't get sidetracked and asked again would you please forgive me for what I had said? They then said, *that yes, that they would forgive me,* and we got things straightened out.

Oh, the flesh hates that! But afterwards there are joy bells ringing in your soul knowing that it has all been resolved.

The other thing that I think of when in this situation is the promise: "For whosoever exalteth himself shall be abased; and he that humbleth himself shall be exalted." (Luke 14:11) That is a promise from God. If you will humble yourself and repent, then you will be exalted, and that exaltation is by the Lord. When the Lord exalts you it is good. If you try to exalt yourself you are going to have trouble.

This modern Christianity has removed repentance, but repentance is biblical. The Lord said, "I say unto you, that likewise joy shall be in heaven over one sinner that repenteth, more than over ninety and nine just persons, which need no repentance." (Luke 15:7)

If you are saved and reading this, then there was a time when you had a change of mind about yourself and about your relation to the God of the universe. You then acted upon your repentance and called upon Jesus Christ to forgive you and to save you from your sins.

Repentance is a requirement for reconciliation. It is very important to realize this. If there is no repentance, then there will be no reconciliation with God, or with your fellow man. Consider the following true story that happened to my wife, Terri.

My wife was raised with a Lutheran/Roman Catholic background. Consequently she was lost. In both of those churches she had never heard the true gospel presented, nor had she ever been presented with the need to be born again.

As a teenager in High School, she had a boyfriend who was a backslidden Christian, and his father was a pastor. The young man had a previous girlfriend whom Terri faked a salvation prayer with when she met her at church. But that event got her going to the Baptist church, and then going over to the pastor's house to see her boyfriend.

After visiting at the house for a couple weeks, one afternoon the pastor's wife took Terri into their bedroom and knelt at the bed with her. She then explained slowly the plan of salvation. Of how Jesus Christ died on the cross to pay for her sins and that if she would call upon Jesus Christ to save her that she would be saved.

To this day Terri explains that she did not understand what the pastor's wife was talking about. Saved? In her mind she thought, *"But I'm not drowning."* She did not understand what being saved meant, even though the pastor's wife explained to her about Hell, and going to Hell if you are not saved. Confusion still filled her mind, yet Terri and the pastor's wife prayed.

Terri prayed out loud and asked Jesus Christ to forgive her of her sins, and to come into her heart and save her. But she did not get saved. Did she call upon the name of the Lord? Yes! Was the plan of salvation explained to her? Yes! Did she get saved? No! If you ask her, she will plainly tell you that she knows that she did not get saved then.

Since Terri had prayed the prayer though, the people around her kind of backed off assuming that she was now saved. This gave her some time to listen to the sermons, as well as it gave time for the Holy Spirit to work on her.

Then one Sunday evening service in February 1979 she heard the pastor preach a message on the White Throne Judgement. For the first time she understood what they had been trying to explain to her. She understood that she was lost and on her way to Hell. But she was afraid to go forward in the invitation because she knew everyone thought that she was saved, and she knew that she wasn't. Right then as that thought went through her mind, the pastor said, *"You don't even have to come forward. You can pray and ask the Lord to save you right there in your seat."*

She bowed her head and prayed right there knowing that she was guilty and lost and on her way to Hell. She prayed and asked Jesus Christ to forgive her of her sins and to come into her heart and to save her. If you ever have the opportunity to ask her, she will tell you that is when and where she got saved.

What is the difference? Repentance! The prayer two weeks earlier was the right prayer but the wrong heart. This time she prayed with a repentant heart and truly got saved.

I was in a church one time where one of the men in the church was getting upset by the preaching. (I was not the one preaching. It was the pastor of the church and he was doing a great job.) During the preaching the man stood up in the middle of the congregation and tried to rebuke the pastor for what he was preaching. The pastor told him that he was out of order and to sit down. He also told him that he owed him an apology. The man shot back sarcastically, *"Well, I'm sorry."* To which the pastor replied, *"That is no apology!"*

Some days went by and the Holy Spirit got to dealing with the man about what he had done. One moring he went to the church and with genuine tears, he went in to see the pastor and asked him for forgiveness for his outburst. The pastor readily forgave him and they got things fixed up.

An apology as a result of repentance is genuine. An apology without repentance is a farce. It is fake. This is a delicate thing though, for people do things differently. Don't sit in judgement on it, for you do not know the heart. You may look for tears when there are none, yet the repentance and asking for forgiveness are real. There is no exact reaction that must take place. "And if he trespass against thee seven times in a day, and seven times in a day turn again to thee, saying, I repent; thou shalt forgive him." (Luke 17:4)

Seven times in a day? That is about once every three hours. In a situation like that it would be very easy to say the repentance is not genuine, but obviously the word of God says that it is.

I have no doubt that there is many a husband or wife, who has been married to a drunk and after they sober up they weep and ask for forgiveness. After five years, ten years or more, it could get to a point where a person doesn't believe it is genuine.

But in Luke 17 it is a saved person, a brother. There are many saved people who have various sins that they haven't got the victory over yet, whether it be booze, drugs, or other sins. The Bible states that if they were to come to you seven times in a day and say, "I repent;" then "thou shalt forgive him."

True repentance will cause a person to seek forgiveness. It will cause you to want to do what you need to in order to make things right whether it is before God or man. To make things right requires *both sides* to do what is required of them.

Concerning these subjects of transgressions, rebuke, and repentance, there is something at the heart of it all and that is the division. Where once two people were close, or at least friendly towards each other, now they are at enmity with one another. It has to do with division, and division often times takes place in homes and amongst families. Perhaps it is a physical family or a spiritual family such as a church, but often times the hurt and pain is felt among families.

> Luke 12:51 Suppose ye that I am come to give peace on earth? I tell you, Nay; but rather division:
>
> 52 For from henceforth there shall be five in one house divided, three against two, and two against three.
>
> 53 The father shall be divided against the son, and the son against the father; the mother against the daughter, and the daughter against the mother; the mother in law against her daughter in law, and the daughter in law against her mother in law.

It seems so strange to read the above scripture. It does not seem to be proper, yet the Lord Jesus Christ said that one of the reasons He came was to bring division, and the division that He is referring to has to do with the family.

Why would He do that? Why would Jesus Christ come to bring division in a family? I believe the answer is: "He that loveth father or mother more than me is not worthy of me: and he that loveth son or daughter more than me is not worthy of me." (Matt. 10:37)

The Lord Jesus Christ, the One who died on the cross and dipped His soul into Hell for you, wants to know if He is first in your heart. Is Jesus Christ more important to you than your own flesh and blood?

For many people He is not! But the Lord bought you with His blood. The Bible says, "For ye are bought with a price..." (1 Cor. 6:20) Jesus Christ owns you and has the right to your unwavering allegience. Unfortunately many people will not choose Jesus Christ over their own family.

Perhaps they will seek a compromise or try to figure out some way to "keep the peace." But in order to keep the peace the Lord has set things up in such a way that you will have to choose one or the other. If you side with Jesus Christ, then it is war with your loved ones. If you go against your Saviour you can have peace and keep the family together without fighting.

If you live for the Lord Jesus Christ and put Him

first, then it is likely that trouble is going to spring up in your family. It doesn't matter if you are a parent or a child, it is likely that trouble is going to spring up. Why? Because Jesus Christ said that was one of the reasons He came. It was to bring division according to Luke 12:51. Now either you believe that or you don't. When the division arises, what are you going to do?

Over the years I have had parents come to me who are having trouble with their children. These are parents who are trying to put Jesus Christ first. They greatly love their children, pray for them, play with them, spend time with them and try to please them as best they can. As the children grow up, they often resent church and the things of God. After years of love and time spent with their children the children get a bad attitude.

I know a man who had to say to his daughter that he loved her, but that he loved Jesus Christ more than her. She was pushing him and testing him over and over to the point that he had to let her know how it was going to go if she kept on.

A lady came to Terri and said that her seventeen-year old son said to her that she loved Jesus Christ more than she loved him, so he was "out of there" and left.

I remember years ago being in a church. It was the first time that I had a meeting there. We pulled into the church parking lot with our RV and were setting up, but I noticed that the pastor seemed to be troubled. I asked him if everything was OK. He told me the following story.

He said to me, *"Last night about 2:00A.M. I got a phone call from the police department. They asked if I was the pastor of the church to which I replied, 'Yes.'"* (I will generalize for the sake of privacy.) *"They then told me that they had my sixteen year old son there at the station. He said he was leaving and had some bags of clothes with him."* The police told this pastor's son that they could not stop him, but that they would contact his parents before they let him go.

The pastor said that he and his wife jumped in the car and drove down there to see his son. He told me that when they arrived at the police station, his wife, the boy's mother, got on her knees, heart broken, and with tears in her eyes, begged for him to come home. She told him that she did not want to see him leave. The boy was hard and didn't flinch. With a cold, stern voice he replied, *"No mom, I will not come home. I am leaving."* And so he did leave.

I remember that the pastor, as he finished telling me the story, he kind of stared downward at the ground, and as he did he said, *"You know, I did more for that boy than I did for all of my other children."* And then with a discouraged, hurt look of frustration, he said, *"But it didn't matter. No matter what I did, it was never enough."*

Before the Pilgrims left for America in the early 1600's, they were living in Holland. After a year or so of living there, they were concerned about their children, for they saw the effect of the worldly ways of Holland on their children. Many of the kids didn't want to leave, and some even stayed when it came time to leave for America. There was a division in their families concerning the worldliness of their children clear back in the early 1600's. Sound familiar?

There are hurts and divisions that happen in families. Often times in Christian homes it is due to, or at least associated with, the Bible and living for Jesus Christ. Though the one hurt, or sinned against has nothing to be ashamed of or to apologize for, yet the longing for that togetherness can move them to apologize when they have nothing to apologize for. Have you ever done that? I ask that question and most often adults will say yes, they have done that.

There is such a desire for reconciliation that there is a hope if you apologize, it might get the ball rolling so to speak, and then the one that is in the wrong will repent and ask for forgiveness. Usually that does not happen.

When you apologize to the one who has done you wrong, even though you do not have anything to apologize for, it has the opposite effect of what you are hoping for. You hope that they, too, will repent and ask for forgiveness. In reality what happens is that your apology reinforces in their mind that they are right, and that you are wrong, when just the opposite is true.

I am not trying to guilt you, for I have done this

very thing. You want so much for forgiveness and reconciliation that you apologize when you have nothing to apologize for. It doesn't work.

You may ask then, *"What do you do in those circumstances?"* You make sure that you have done what the Lord wants you to do. Beyond that, you pray about it. Then you must go on and serve your Saviour. What else can you do?

Reconciliation requires *both sides* doing what they are supposed to do. On the one side, you have the one that has been trespassed against. They confront the trespassor and rebuke them. *If there is no repentance, then there can be no reconciliation.* That's how it works with the Lord.

A sinner trespasses against the Lord. He rebukes them and lets them know that they have done wrong. When they do not repent, He waits.

But God is prevented from proceeding any farther because there is a lack of repentance on the one guilty. Does the Lord desire to be reconciled to them? No doubt! "The Lord is not slack concerning his promise, as some men count slackness; but is longsuffering to us-ward, not willing that any should perish, but that all should come to repentance." (2 Pet. 3:9) But God will not step over man's free will, contrary to what John Calvin taught. *Reconciliation can only proceed if there is repentance on the part of the guilty.* That is true between God and man, and that is true between person to person.

If you seek peace without repentance then you

will have to go contrary to the direct will of God. In such situations in order to bring about peace and unity, you will have to turn your back on your Saviour. Do not do that! That makes your family an idol. Jesus Christ is to be first. What's more is that the "peace and unity" will be fake. You have not sought it God's way.

Chapter 5
Forgive

Eph 4:32 ...Even as God for Christ's sake hath forgiven you.

The Bible states in Ephesians 4:32 that God is our example of forgiveness. There is no one more forgiving than our Lord Jesus Christ. The apostle Paul said that he was the chiefest of sinners, and the Lord forgave him. There is testimony after testimony of people who were Satanists, and they got saved. Here is just one example.

David Berkowitz, aka Son of Sam, serial murderer, Interviewed by Scott Ross of CBN:

"I at one time had gotten into Satan worship. And this entity, this demon, that was his name. It was just the stupidest thing I had ever done in my life. I just let the devil take control of me. And back in

1975, '76, even before the crimes started, I made a pact with the devil.

I wanted to get delivered. I wanted to get delivered. I was living without hope. I had surrendered myself to ... to serve the devil.

Well, the past, the scars of the past are always going to remain and haunt me. But I've given my life to Jesus Christ. And He has let me know in His Word that He has forgiven me completely. All my sins are washed away."

(http://www1.cbn.com/700club/son-sam-becomes-son-hope)

In the book of Exodus, chapter 33 - 34, Moses comes down from getting the Ten Commandments on Mt. Sinai and beholds Israel dancing naked around a golden calf. Furious at the sight, he throws the tablets down on the ground and they break.

You can read it for yourself, but let me make a long story short. As the Lord talks to Moses in the tabernacle, Moses asks Him, "I beseech thee, shew me thy glory." (Ex. 33:18)

> Ex. 33:20 And he said, Thou canst not see my face: for there shall no man see me, and live.
>
> 22 "...while my glory passeth by, that I will put thee in a clift of the rock, and will cover thee with my hand while I pass by:"

The Lord put Moses in the clift of the rock and after covering his face, the Lord passed by and proclaimed this about himself:

> Ex. 34:6 And the LORD passed by before him, and proclaimed, The LORD, The LORD God, merciful and gracious, longsuffering, and abundant in goodness and truth,
> 7 Keeping mercy for thousands, forgiving iniquity and transgression and sin, and that will by no means clear *the guilty*; visiting the iniquity of the fathers upon the children, and upon the children's children, unto the third and to the fourth *generation*.

The Lord is a very forgiving God as you can see from the Scriptures. But He is also a balanced God, with what is written about him in the last half of those two verses. To be all forgiving without the part where He states, "and that will be no means clear *the guilty*" is to be unbalanced.

The modern view of God is a perverted view. The common portrayal of God today is not a portrait that even remotely resembles the God of the Bible. The modern portrait is one of all love, all forgiving and kind. The attributes that would appear negative towards man are ignored or altogether left out.

To those who are living for themselves, apart from any attempt to please their Creator, they will emphasize how loving God is, and how forgiving God is. The reason they do this is because they are living wrong and wickedly contrary to the express will and word of God, and they know it.

This is one of the reasons the symbol of the Sodomites is a rainbow. Where did the rainbow come from? What does it symbolize?

> Gen. 9:11 And I will establish my covenant with you; neither shall all flesh be cut off any more by the waters of a flood; neither shall there any more be a flood to destroy the earth.
>
> 12 And God said, This *is* the token of the covenant which I make between me and you and every living creature that *is* with you, for perpetual generations
>
> 13 I do set my bow in the cloud, and it shall be for a token of a covenant between me and the earth.

God set the rainbow in the cloud as a token that He will never destroy the earth again with a flood of waters. The flood was a judgement upon all flesh for the wickedness that mankind was committing, and God used the flood to wipe them out. The "bow," or what we call the rainbow, is the symbol that God will not do that again.

So the Sodomites have unconsciously adopted

that as their symbol, and in a sense are holding it before God as they live wickedly. It is true that God will not ever destroy the earth again with a flood. The next time He is going to melt it with fire. "But the day of the Lord will come as a thief in the night; in the which the heavens shall pass away with a great noise, and the elements shall melt with fervent heat, the earth also and the works that are therein shall be burned up." (2 Pet. 3:10)

Nevertheless, there are many stories and verses in the word of God that shew God as a loving and forgiving God. Before God, who is the Lord Jesus Christ, ever gets to the point of judgement there have been a long series of attempts, initiated by Him, to be reconciled to His creation.

In this story I just referenced about Noah and the world wide flood, God used Noah to warn the people for one hundred and twenty years before the judgement fell. Noah was a preacher and warned them. "And spared not the old world, but saved Noah the eighth *person*, a preacher of righteousness, bringing in the flood upon the world of the ungodly." (2Pet. 2:5) God warned them, but eventually the judgement came.

There is another example in the Bible of how God warns the wicked of what He is getting ready to do. The story is about a woman, an harlot, named Rahab.

Joshua and the nation of Israel were getting ready to attack Jericho and to destroy it, according to the commandment of God. It was a wicked city and God was bringing judgement upon it. Inside the city the people knew what God was getting ready to do, yet only one person repented and acted by faith, and it was the harlot, Rahab. Notice the amount of light she had, and what she states, every else had to know.

> Josh. 2:8 And before they were laid down, she came up unto them upon the roof;
> 9 And she said unto the men, I know that the LORD hath given you the land, and that your terror is fallen upon us, and that all the inhabitants of the land faint because of you.
> 10 For we have heard how the LORD dried up the water of the Red sea for you, when ye came out of Egypt; and what ye did unto the two kings of the Amorites, that *were* on the other side Jordan, Sihon and Og, whom ye utterly destroyed.
> 11 And as soon as we had heard *these things*, our hearts did melt, neither did there remain any more courage in any man, because of you: for the LORD your God, he *is* God in heaven above, and in earth beneath.

They had light and time to repent.
The Lord is ready to forgive, He wants to forgive,

but as I have already covered, *there is no forgiveness without repentance.*

Consider the great city of Nineveh. It was living very wickedly and God was getting ready to destroy it. But God does not want to destroy it, so He calls a man by the name of Jonah to go and preach to the people in the city.

The man Jonah does not want to go so he runs from the Lord. You can read the story for yourself in the Bible, for it is not long. Jonah eventually obeys God and goes to the city and preaches, "Yet forty days, and Nineveh shall be overthrown." (Jonah 3:4) That is all he says. It is one of the shortest messages ever delivered by a preacher, yet the whole city repents. The word of God says,

> "And God saw their works, that they turned from their evil way; and God repented of the evil, that he had said that he would do unto them; and he did *it* not." (Jonah 3:10)

It is God's desire to forgive. He delights in forgiveness. He does not enjoy destruction.

Jonah gets upset with the Lord because he does not destroy Nineveh. They were the enemies of Israel. Notice the heart of God by what He replies to Jonah:

> "And should not I spare Nineveh, that great city, wherein are more than sixscore

> thousand persons that cannot discern between their right hand and their left hand; and *also* much cattle? (Jonah 4:11)

When I think of forgiveness in the word of God I think of the story of the Prodigal Son. In my opinion, it is one of the greatest stories concerning forgiveness in all of the Bible .

"Then drew near unto him all the publicans and sinners for to hear him." (Luke 15:1) These were the down and out class. The people that today would be the druggies, drunks, prostitutes, gang members and such like. The Lord Jesus Christ tells them a great story about the forgiveness of God.

In case you don't have a Bible handy I am going to include the story. I thought about freely telling the story, but there is no substitute for the word of God. Perhaps you have read it many times before, but read it one more time slowly, and then think about the time that you came home to the Father and how He had been looking, longing and waiting for you. Think about how there was no hesitation from Him, when you called upon His name and believed on the Lord Jesus Christ as your personal Saviour, and that He FORGAVE YOU. Through Jesus Christ, if you are saved, all of your sins have been forgiven. You are forgiven. That is something you need to stop and think about now and then.

Luke 15:11 ¶ And he said, A certain man had two sons:

Luke 15:12 And the younger of them said to *his* father, Father, give me the portion of goods that falleth *to me*. And he divided unto them *his* living.

Luke 15:13 And not many days after the younger son gathered all together, and took his journey into a far country, and there wasted his substance with riotous living.

Luke 15:14 And when he had spent all, there arose a mighty famine in that land; and he began to be in want.

Luke 15:15 And he went and joined himself to a citizen of that country; and he sent him into his fields to feed swine.

Luke 15:16 And he would fain have filled his belly with the husks that the swine did eat: and no man gave unto him.

Luke 15:17 And when he came to himself, he said, How many hired servants of my father's have bread enough and to spare, and I perish with hunger!

Luke 15:18 I will arise and go to my father, and will say unto him, Father, I have sinned against heaven, and before thee,

Luke 15:19 And am no more worthy to be called thy son: make me as one of thy hired servants.

Luke 15:20 And he arose, and came to his father. But when he was yet a great way off, his father saw him, and had compassion, and ran, and fell on his neck, and kissed him.

Luke 15:21 And the son said unto him, Father, I have sinned against heaven, and in thy sight, and am no more worthy to be called thy son.

Luke 15:22 But the father said to his servants, Bring forth the best robe, and put *it* on him; and put a ring on his hand, and shoes on *his* feet:

Luke 15:23 And bring hither the fatted calf, and kill *it*; and let us eat, and be merry:

Luke 15:24 For this my son was dead, and is alive again; he was lost, and is found. And they began to be merry.

When the prodigal son got ready to come home he was repentant and broken. "And am no more worthy to be called thy son." (Luke 15:19) He knew that he was not worthy to be called his father's son anymore, and it seems from the passage that he is merely hoping to become one of the servants. But what he under estimated was the love, the compassion, and forgiveness of his father. The father did not go after the son, but the father longed to see him again and he was watching for the day his son would come home.

The father in the story is a picture of God the Father. That picture shows a father who is waiting for his son to return home. He could not go after his son because the only way he could ever be reconciled to his son would be if his son repents, comes home and asks for forgiveness. The father longs to forgive but cannot until his son repents and then asks for forgiveness. Isn't that how you got saved? Isn't that how you got right with God?

"When he (the son) was yet a great way off." The father's eyesight was really good. He saw far out in the distance long before the son would hold his head up high enough to see the old home stead. It was the father of the prodigal that came running to meet him, and he was ready to forgive his son and welcome him home, not as a servant, but as his son. One of the great truths of the story of the prodigal son is the story of forgiveness.

I am so glad for the day that I realized that I was not worthy to go to Heaven. I realized that I was a sinner and guilty before God, and what I needed was forgiveness. I did not need a new life, or a reformation. I needed to be forgiven by my Creator, for I had sinned against Him. I was guilty and deserving of Hell, but thank God for the night that I knelt beside my bed, closed my eyes and began to pray. I didn't know how to pray, I didn't know theology, and I didn't know a lot of things. But that night as I prayed I asked Jesus Christ to forgive me of my sins and to come into my heart and save me. And Jesus Christ forgave me, washed me from my sins in his own blood and clothed me in a new robe of God's righteousness.

When it comes to the subject of forgiveness then, the greatest example and the greatest place, is the story of the cross. There are many things about our God that are great. Our God, the Lord Jesus Christ, is the Most High God. In other words there is no god as high as Jesus Christ. Not only that, but the Lord Jesus Christ is Holy. There is no spot, no blemish, no sin, no darkness in Him at all, for He is light. "This then is the message which we have heard of him, and declare unto you, that God is light, and in him is no darkness at all." (1John 1:5) The Lord Jesus Christ is eternal, all knowing, all powerful and "His mouth *is* most sweet: yea, he *is* altogether lovely. This *is* my beloved, and this *is* my friend." (Song of Solomon 5:16) But as a sinner and guilty before the Holy God of the universe, the Lord Jesus Christ, I am so thankful that He is a forgiving God!

I am thankful that He is ready and willing to forgive sinners. Not only is He ready and willing, but He is longing for sinners to come to Him repenting of their sins. He is eager to answer those who call upon the Lord Jesus Christ to forgive them of their sins and to make them fit for Heaven. There is no other way to Heaven than through the Lord Jesus Christ. He freely forgives once your heart responds to Him by faith.

You do not get saved in your head, but you get saved in your heart. It is not merely the knowledge of God and what He did on the cross, but it is realizing that when He died on the cross He was dying for you. I mean you, dear reader, right now as you read this, know that Jesus Christ died on the cross for YOU! He died so that you could be forgiven of your sins and go to Heaven when you die.

For sinners, the greatest story in the word of God is the old old story of Jesus and His love. He desires to forgive you, just like the father of the prodigal longed to forgive his son and to welcome him home. His forgiveness is freely given or bestowed upon those who repent (I am not worthy) and call, or believe on the Lord Jesus Christ.

What does it mean to be forgiven? In regards to God it has to do with no longer being under His wrath. The Bible states, "...he that believeth not the Son shall not see life; but the wrath of God abideth on Him." (John 3:36) The Bible states that, "...God is angry *with the wicked* every day." (Psalms 7:11) I covered this in the chapter on having transgressed against the Lord.

The acts that you did to make God mad, and that caused you to be a transgressor and guilty before God, no longer make God mad, because He has forgiven you. He promises to forgive all who will repent and call upon the Lord Jesus Christ. "For whosoever shall call upon the name of the Lord shall be saved." (Rom. 10:13)

It is as if you owed a debt to God, and the debt was growing bigger each day because each day you kept breaking the commandments of God. The only way those debts could be paid was by the shedding of God's blood (Acts 20:28 *KJV) for without the shedding of blood there is no remission of sin. But when you realized that you were guilty before God and deserved Hell, and that Jesus Christ died for you and paid for your sins, you then called upon the Lord Jesus Christ and asked Him to forgive you of your sins. All of those sins are forgiven. God is no longer angry with you because He has forgiven you. Stop and think about that for awhile!

I have gone into this quite a bit so that you will have an understanding of the best examples of forgiveness there are in the word of God. The Lord Jesus Christ himself, is the best example of forgiveness there is. To that there is no doubt, and for you and I the Bible tells us that we are to forgive, "...even as God for Christ' sake hath forgiven you." (Eph 4:33) He is our example when it comes to forgiving each other.

As our example then, you must understand that when someone comes to Jesus Christ realizing that they have sinned against Him and are guilty, that when they call upon the Lord Jesus Christ for forgiveness, He immediately forgives them. He does not delay, for He is longing to forgive them. He does not reply to the call for salvation, *"Well, I'll think about it!"* No, He is ready to forgive and does forgive without hesitation, and you should be that way as well.

But what happens if a brother or sister has trespassed against you, and they have not come to you for forgiveness? What do you do if you have been trespassed against, you have rebuked them, and they have not repented? How do you deal with that?

> Matt. 6:14 For if ye forgive men their trespasses, your heavenly Father will also forgive you
> 15 But if ye forgive not men their trespasses, neither will your Father forgive your trespasses.

> Mark 11:25 And when ye stand praying, forgive, if ye have ought against any: that your Father also which is in heaven may forgive you your trespasses.
> 26 But if ye do not forgive, neither will your Father which is in heaven forgive your trespasses.

There is no doubt based upon the scriptures that I just cited that we are to forgive if we have ought against any, but does this mean that we are to continue as if nothing ever happened? That would contradict Ephesians 4:32, "...even as God."

This is where the world, and the worldly Christians come along and say that you are to forgive and you should never have ought against any of your brethren. While that is true according to Mark 11:25 “And when ye stand praying, forgive, if ye have ought against any...,” yet how do you deal with that if a brother or sister comes along and spits in your face, steals your car, or lies about you to many people. Are you to forgive and act like it never happened? If you think so, then what about Luke 17:3-4? Why would you go to them and rebuke them? If thy brother trespass against thee, rebuke him; and if he repent, forgive him.

If you are to forgive them and act like nothing ever happened, then is that how God is? Is that how God forgives? No, that is not how God forgives, and that is not how God reacts when someone sins against Him, whether they are saved or lost. In regards to the lost, let me tell you a true story that was told to me by the man in the story.

He was a soldier with the United States Army. He was saved and a good witness for the Lord Jesus Christ while in the Army, which is not easy to do. He was stationed in Iraq at the time the following events took place. I will call him Jim. This story is about four lost fellow soldiers and how they died.

Jim had been in many firefights with the enemy. He also had won a number of his fellow soldiers to a saving knowledge of the Lord Jesus Christ. One day back in the camp Jim was witnessing to a soldier, and the Holy Spirit seemed to be working and bringing conviction upon the fellow comrade when another soldier walked by who was a Muslim. The Muslim spoke up and ruined the witness from proceeding any further. He said in a mocking way something to the effect that Jesus didn't rise from the dead and He wasn't God.

Another soldier that Jim had witnessed to professed to be a Buddhist. Jim told him how Jesus Christ was the true God, rose from the dead and died for his sins on the cross. The Buddhist laughed and mocked at what Jim told him.

There was another soldier who was always drinking booze. He loved to get drunk and would be out drinking whenever he could. Jim told him how he needed to repent. How that wine was a mocker and strong drink was raging, yet this soldier cussed him out and told him to shut up.

The last soldier was a fornicator, and a womanizer. He would brag about the women he had been with. One day Jim told him that what he was doing was not right in the sight of God. He told him that he ought to get married for that was God's approved way of satisfaction. This wicked man also didn't listen and mocked what Jim had told him.

Early one morning as the men were putting on their gear and getting ready to go out on patrol, the Muslim soldier dropped over dead. He just fell over dead. They did an autopsy on him and could find no cause of death. Jim told me that the

Muslim's head hit the floor and cracked open, but hardly any blood came out. For that to happen the heart had to have been stopped completely.

The Buddhist was standing not far away from a tank when a missile went off beside him and vaporized him. Jim said there was literally nothing left of him but a small bit of burnt blood on the side of the tank.

Both of those incidents happened not too long after Jim had witnessed to both of them, and what's more, his fellow soldiers all knew that Jim had just witnessed to them.

Then as they were out on patrol a bullet came through the windshield of a Humvee, went through the mouth of the boozer and killed him.

The last solder, who was the fornicating womanizer was out on patrol riding in a Humvee. A bullet ricocheted off the road from underneath the Humvee and came up through the bottom of the Humvee, piercing his privates between his legs and causing him to bleed to death before they could get help for him.

Jim's fellow soldiers all knew that he had witnessed to all four of these men, and they were very aware of how each one died because the deaths were so out of the norm. He told me that the other soldiers began to walk cautiously around him. That is just four examples that God is very aware of all things and will deal with such as He so desires.

It has been said that light rejected becomes

lightning. That is so true for these four men who rejected the truth. The Lord God was longing and waiting for them to repent. They mocked and rejected Jesus Christ, and He decided *"I've put up with you long enough."*

To those reading this that are saved, there are certain things that took place when you got saved that will never change. These things have to do with your standing in Christ. Your standing in Christ will never change.

When you were born again you were regenerated by the Spirit of God. You were born spiritually and that will never change. "...Unto him that loved us, and washed us from our sins in his own blood." (Rev 1:5) You were washed in the blood of Jesus Christ. "And grieve not the holy Spirit of God, whereby ye are sealed unto the day of redemption." (Eph. 4:30) You are sealed by the Holy Spirit. You become a child of God (John 1:12) and your name is written in the book of life. (Phil. 4:3) You are baptized into Jesus Christ (1 Cor. 12:13) and you are accepted in the beloved (Eph. 1:6), and these things will never change. You will not lose your salvation because of your sinning against God, whether you sin against Him a lot or a little.

> Rom. 8:38 For I am persuaded, that neither death, nor life, nor angels, nor principalities, nor powers, nor things present, nor things to come,

> 39 Nor height, nor depth, nor any other creature, shall be able to separate us from the love of God, which is in Christ Jesus our Lord.

I had to put those verses in as they are two great verses!

Do we all sin every day? Yes! "If we say that we have no sin, we deceive ourselves, and the truth is not in us." (1 John 1:8) Yes, we sin every day, but do your sins bother you? "If we confess our sins, he is faithful and just to forgive us *our* sins, and to cleanse us from all unrighteousness." (1 John 1:9) If you are saved then you should be trying to do right and to live a clean and Godly life each day. God is watching you, for "The eyes of the Lord *are* in every place, beholding the evil and the good." (Prov. 15:3) There ought to be a desire to please Him, and you know that when you sin it does not please Him. With this in mind, you should go to Jesus Christ and confess your sins before Him.

Some Christians don't care if they sin against their Saviour. Yes, they are saved, born again, redeemed by the blood of the Lamb, but they don't care if they sin against God. Who would be like that? Well, someone who is mad at God. Or someone who has become discouraged and quit trying to live for the Lord. There are any number of reasons why Christians get to the point where they don't care if they are sinning against their

Lord and Saviour.

How does Jesus Christ respond to someone like this? What happens between a Christian, who is carelessly sinning, and their Saviour? What happens is that the Holy Spirit is grieved, quenched, and Jesus Christ is no longer as close to them as He used to be. The fellowship between the Christian and their Saviour is broken. Are they still saved? Of course they are! Are they in fellowship with their Saviour? No!

I don't want to get off track and cover the subject with regard to the chastening hand of God. But suffice it to say that the Lord Jesus Christ will rebuke, chasten, and even kill a backslidden Christian if they will not repent and get right with Him. He does not continue on like nothing is wrong, just the opposite is true.

I have already covered this, so just a brief review as it is very important.

Are you to continue on like nothing is wrong when someone has, or is sinning or trespassing against you? No! But you are to forgive them. What I mean is that you are to forgive them between you and your Saviour. This is Heavenward.

Don't let what others do against you cause you to lose your fellowship with your Saviour. You have got to forgive them before God. Forgiveness is a choice and you must choose to forgive them between you and God. That does not mean that your relationship between you and them on this earth is to be like nothing ever happened. What it means is that you are not to get bitter, angry and agitated against them, thus causing thoughts of revenge upon them. Those thoughts grieve the Spirit of God that dwells in your body.

You are to forgive them, but there is a difference between forgiveness and reconciliation. Just because you have forgiven them does not mean that you are to act like nothing ever happened, or that all is right between you and them. That is not Bible.

I am talking about forgiving before they have ever come to you and asked you for forgiveness. *You must realize that they may never come to you and ask for forgiveness.* You cannot, you must not, hold on to your anger and hurt for it will turn into bitterness. When that happens, you will have broken your fellowship with God, and Satan will have the victory in your trial.

You must forgive them in your heart before God. Stop and realize, are we all sinners? Yes! All of our flesh is depraved. We have an old man that is corrupt, and we all give into our old man sooner or later. But by the grace of God, there go I. Forgive them in your heart and move on.

By doing this, if they ever do come to you repentant and ask for your forgiveness, then it will be easy to forgive them. If you don't forgive them between you and God, then the wound will fester and get worse. If that happens, then if they come to you and ask for forgiveness, it will be almost impossible for you to forgive them. Don't do that.

Remember, if you got what you deserve you would be in Hell. The Lord Jesus Christ has been better to you than you deserve. By His grace choose to forgive them, and don't let what they did to hurt you cause you to lose your walk and fellowship with God. Guard you heart and keep your fellowship with your Saviour right.

After you forgive them, you are to go to them and rebuke them. That is not easy to do, but you are commanded by God to do that. And let me say here that your rebuke ought to be with charity. You don't have to go angry, yelling at them, and you shouldn't go that way. But in the spirit of meekness you are to rebuke them and let them know what they did wrong.

If they do come to you and ask for forgiveness you are to forgive them.

> Luke 17:3 Take heed to yourselves: If thy brother trespass against thee, rebuke him; and if he repent, forgive him.
>
> 4 And if he trespass against thee seven times in a day, and seven times in a day turn again to thee, saying, I repent; thou shalt forgive him.

If they come to you seven times in a day, about once every three hours, then you are to forgive them. That would be hard to do. I would think that after the fourth or fifth time I would be thinking that the apologies were not genuine, but the Bible says to forgive them.

Forgiveness is the key that unlocks the prison door of resentment and breaks the shackles of hate. It is the power that breaks the chains of bitterness.

If you are trespassed against seven times in a day, I wonder if you rebuke them seven times in that day? My guess is, yes, you would.

I know of more than one case where a husband has gotten saved and asked his wife for forgiveness for the way he treated her. Compared to the world, these men did not treat their wives badly. They did not beat them, nor were they unfaithful to them. They worked, paid the bills and even when they were lost, they loved their wives. In these cases the saved wives would not forgive their newly saved, babes in the Lord, husbands. In such cases, the wives are the ones that are now wrong.

If someone does you wrong, then they are wrong. If someone does you wrong, you then rebuke them and when they come to you and ask for forgiveness, and you don't forgive them, now you are wrong. If you "can't" or don't forgive them it is due to your pride, and you are not right with God!

It has been said that we are like beasts when we kill. We are like men when we judge. We are like God when we forgive. If anyone should be able to forgive it should be God's people.

You may have hurt someone and you know it. Maybe they rebuked you or maybe they didn't, but you know that you have hurt them. You have gone to them and apologized to them and have sought their forgiveness, but they will not forgive you. What can you do in that situation? You have done what you can, and you have done what the Bible tells you to do. Make sure all is right between you and God, then go on and serve your Lord Jesus Christ. There is nothing else you can do but to pray for them.

They may bring it up on occasion and use it against you. If the Lord allows you to, remind them that you apologized to them about it. In such a situation you are going to have to go to the Lord and pray about it. Tell Him how you feel, tell Him about your frustration, and tell Him everything. The place to go is to your Saviour and the word of God.

I have a couple people whom I have gone to and apologized. Whether I truly had done wrong to them I wonder, but in their minds I did, so I have apologized to them. Both of them have not forgiven me, and both of them have said things to others about me. As best as I know how, I have done what the Lord Jesus Christ commanded me to do. Beyond that I must pray, move on and serve Him. In order for each of those relationships to be restored, there must be forgiveness, which I have asked for on their part, and they won't forgive. That is beyond my control. I have done my part.

Many a marriage could be sweet and a little bit of Heaven on earth but for one spouse who, though they have been apologized to and asked to forgive, yet they will not forgive. It doesn't matter if it is a husband or wife, some people do not want to forgive. They will hang on to the hurt seeking to inflict pain on their spouse, and they will reap what they sow.

"Forgiveness is an act of the will regardless of the temperature of the heart." Corrie Ten Boom

Chapter 6
Reconcile

> Eph. 4:32 And be ye kind one to another, tenderhearted, forgiving one another, even as God for Christ's sake hath forgiven you.

The last thing that happened when God forgave you was that you were reconciled to Him. Where once you were alienated from God and under His wrath, and there was enmity between you and Him, now you are reconciled. You and the God of this universe are now at peace between the both of you. You have been reconciled and *brought into agreement* where once there was disagreement and division.

In order for reconciliation to take place there has to be action from the people on *both sides* of the division. The transgressor must repent, and the one transgressed against must forgive. If one side does not, or will not, do their duty, then *reconciliation cannot take place.*

This is very important to understand because the common misconception in these last days is that Christians are never supposed to be angry, hurt or upset with anyone. And when they are angry, hurt, or upset with someone, then they are not right with God. If they were right with God they would forgive and move on.

Well, yes, you should forgive, between you and God, but that does not mean that you will have any sort of relationship with the offender. The world, and likely the offender, will accuse you of not being a good Christian if you have any division between you and someone else. Of course, they don't live that way, but they will hold you to that standard. But *that is a standard that even God does not go by.*

The worldly Christians that make God sick (Rev. 3) have a messed-up view of what a Christian ought to be. There is this unbiblical attitude that a Christian is a soft-spoken, spineless pushover that never makes anyone mad and who never gets mad at anything. Paul made people mad, Peter made people mad, and many others in the word of God made people mad even though they were doing right. As I have already gone over, there is a legitimate trespass, and one that's not legitimate. When it is a legitimate trespass it is not to be ignored. It is to be dealt with.

God does not ignore the offense and proceed as

if nothing ever happened, but that is what many Christians think is the way they should be. To think this way and to have been trespassed against is very frustrating. You have had a yoke placed upon you that even God Himself does not bear. "For they bind heavy burdens and grievous to be borne, and lay *them* on men's shoulders; but they *themselves* will not move them with one of their fingers." (Matt. 23:4)

There is nothing more frustrating than to have been trespassed against by a loved one only to be accused of being implacable, bitter, and unforgiving because you will not act like nothing ever happened. You are the one that has been betrayed and yet you are the one that continues to be attacked. This is not of God.

Yes, if you are in their presence you can be polite and kind, though this is only because you have forgiven them "Heavenward" between you and the Lord, but "earthward" there is still division. What makes it harder is that in your heart you probably long for reconciliation, but you must realize it takes both parties. If one of the parties will not repent, or forgive, then there will be no reconciliation.

Let's say that you have had your heart broken by a loved one, and you have rebuked them and let them know that they did wrong, but they will not repent of what they did. Maybe they deny it, minimize it, or excuse it to you and others, so there is an obvious division with this loved one. Perhaps there is an obvious division in your family, and there is pressure and accusations that if you would get right with God then all will be well.

You, the one trespassed against, do not, and should not feel guilty, for you did not do wrong. If you *"give in"* then it will be you that has to *"repent"* for not being right with God and being upset. It will be you that has to conceal the hurt. It will be you that is very frustrated with life. And it will be you who has just verified to the one who transgressed against you that they did nothing wrong, which is not the truth.

In these situations mothers have a very hard time holding up. They will break and act like all is well in order to keep the peace. But I know men who are holding the line, and it is not easy. They are viewed as the *"bad guy."* You're just being too extreme. Is there no compromise? You are so hard! On and on go the accusations.

A position where this happens all the time is the pastorate. A pastor has to stand for what is right and the pressure to compromise is extreme. In this age fewer and fewer pastors are holding the line and standing for what is right.

In regards to Luke 12:51-53 and the division that Jesus Christ came to bring, if you are a parent reading this, please take note of what I am saying. If you treated your Saviour the way your child has treated you, what kind of relationship would you have? If you treated your Saviour the way your parents have treated you, what kind of relationship would you have?

If your parents, or children are lost, and you are saved, then you should have more grace with them. God sends His rain on the just and the unjust. God sends His sunshine on the lost and saved. It does not mean that He has a close relationship with them, but He is kind to them and longsuffering, not willing that any should perish but that all should come to repentance.

Situations are different so the main context of this book is divisions between saved people, but it will apply as a general rule for all.

I think of David when he comes to see the battle and Goliath comes out and defies Israel. Eliab, David's oldest brother, by about ten years, comes and berates David to which David says one his most famous statements. "And David said, What have I now done? *Is there* not a cause?" (1Sam. 17:29) What is important though is to notice David's next action, "And he turned from him toward another." (1Sam. 17:30) David was the youngest, and Eliab was the oldest of eight boys, not including sisters of which there were at least two. (1 Chron. 2:16) There was a large age difference between David and Eliab, but David did not hesitate and turned from him toward another and went on to do the work of God. That is what you are going to have to do.

It is a blessing to have a life! What do I mean by that? I mean that if you are saved, then your life is not wrapped up in people. At least it ought not to be. Your life is to be wrapped up in the Lord Jesus Christ and doing His perfect will for your life.

If your life is, or has been wrapped up in people, specifically the one who has trespassed against you, then maybe the Lord has allowed this to happen to you so that you will turn your eyes upon Jesus and what He wants for you. If that is the case, then the "curse" will become a "blessing," for you have been freed up to serve the Lord Jesus Christ and thus hear Him say one day *"Well done, thou good and faithful servant."*

You should remember as well that God understands and knows exactly how you feel and what you are going through. All through the Old Testament God the Father reaches out to Israel only to be rejected. He brings judgment upon them and they repent, for he said: "I will go *and* return to my place, till they acknowledge their offence, and seek my face: in their affliction they will seek me early." (Hos. 5:15) Did you notice what He said, "till they acknowledge their offence." God is waiting for them to repent and will not reconcile until they do, but He is longing for the reconciliation.

> "And they that escape of you shall remember me among the nations whither they shall be carried captives, because I am broken with their whorish heart, which hath departed from me, and with their eyes, which go a whoring after their idols: and they shall lothe themselves for the evils which they have committed in all their abominations." (Ezek. 6:9)

God was broken because of how His people had departed from Him. That is an amazing thing when you stop and thing about it. God the Father, who is all powerful *is broken* because His people have trespassed against Him. He has to wait until they "lothe themselves" before He can be reconciled to them. But what happens is that God turns from Israel during the book of Acts and goes to the Gentiles. *God departs from His people and you may have to do them same.*

Yes, you long for reconciliation! Yes, you long to hear their voice again, to hug them and be at peace once again, but it takes two to be reconciled. The help from understanding "even as God" is that *you do not have to feel guilty for doing right.*

God weeps for His people Israel yet they would not repent. Jesus laments over Jerusalem,

> "O Jerusalem, Jerusalem, which killest the prophets, and stonest them that are sent unto thee; how often would I have gathered thy children together, as a hen doth gather her brood under her wings, and ye would not!" (Luke 13:34)

The Lord desires and longs for reconciliation but Isreal would not repent, "Ye would not."

If you are longing for reconciliation, and you have done all that you can do, then there is nothing more that you can do, except pray. I do not want to minimize prayer, but it takes two parties for reconciliation to take place.

The two parties have a division between them. Something has happened that split them up and ruined the relationship. Whatever is causing the division must be removed in order for the two parties to come back together. To ignore the wedge, or that something that is between the two will only *hurt the one wounded and deceive the offender* into continuing on in their error.

If God was to act like everything was alright between Him and a sinner, or a backslidden Christian, it would cause the sinner to end up in Hell and the Christian would never get right. Not only that, but God would be hypocritical for He would be acting contrary to the truth.

It is the same way with you. If someone has done you wrong, and you continue to act like everything is fine, then that someone will never see the need to repent.

One dark misty night down in Louisiana a preacher was coming home from a meeting. It was actually early morning around 3:00 A.M. and he was driving across a very long bridge. In the South, some of those bridges will be ten miles long, or longer. All was quiet as he drove on in the night. There was almost no one else on the road.

He wasn't traveling all that fast as his headlights tried to cut through the foggy mist. Then through the mist, he thought he saw a man standing in the middle of the bridge. Thinking he was dreaming, he blinked his eyes and looked again. Sure enough it was a man, a wild man, standing in the middle of the road which was also in the middle of nowhere because of how long the bridge was.

He began to slow down as the seemingly deranged man was now in full view. There was no doubt it was a man and he appeared wild. His hair was messed up, his clothes were coming apart, and he was yelling and pointing at the car.

The preacher sat up and his heartbeat hastened. His mind raced as he sent up quick prayers, *"Oh God, help me. What should I do?"* The wild man was standing and yelling right in the middle of the road. The preacher then moved his car over to the other side of the bridge, and the man moved over to that side as well. The preacher then steered his car back to the other side, and the man quickly went to that side as well.

"What should I do, what should I do?" As his mind raced, he decided that when he got closer to the man that he would step on the gas, turn the steering wheel and drive around the wild man.

Slowly approaching ever closer, he then stepped on the gas and turned the steering wheel, only to have the man jump onto the hood of his car. Now he was beating on the windshield and yelling wildly, but it seemed like he was yelling, *"Stop!"* What could he do? The preacher was out of alternatives, so he stopped and cracked his window down ever so slightly. He then nervously said, *"What's wrong?"*

The wild man, gasping for breath, shouted, *"Mister, stop, you have to stop. A barge has crashed into the bridge and a section is completely gone. I went over in my car but was able to climb back up here to warn people of the danger. You are the first car that has arrived."*

The preacher said that he was no longer afraid of the man. As a matter of fact, he now kind of liked the guy. Then he turned his car sideways on the bridge and got out and waited. As the next car approached he was on one side of the bridge, and the man was on the other. Both of them waved their arms, yelled and warned the next car to stop because the bridge was out.

What if they didn't say anything? What if they didn't sound the warning? They would betray their trust.

In regards to repentance, and please don't be discouraged in what I am about to write, but it is the truth so I want to mention it. There is no doubt that God desires to be reconciled to man. "The Lord is not slack concerning his promise, as some men count slackness; but is longsuffering to us-ward, not willing that any should perish, but that all should come to repentance." (2 Pet. 3:9) So the Lord lets man know that he has sinned against God. And God waits, and waits in his longsuffering for men to repent, and you know what? The vast majority of them never do repent. "...broad *is* the way, that leadeth to destruction, and many there be which go in thereat:" (Matt.7:13)

In regards to Christians the Lord says,

> "...The harvest truly is great, but the labourers are few:" (Luke 10:2)
>
> "For many are called, but few *are*

> chosen." (Matt. 22:14)
>
> "These shall make war with the Lamb, and the Lamb shall overcome them: for he is Lord of lords, and King of kings: and they that are with him *are* called, and chosen, and faithful." (Rev. 17:14)

When Jesus Christ ministered on this earth there were the multitudes that came to hear him. Then there were the twelve disciples. Then there were three of the twelve disciples that were close to the Lord: Peter, James and John. And even then there was John, who was that disciple whom Jesus loved.

I am just saying that when it comes to people repenting and getting things right, it is a very few. You must put your eyes on Jesus Christ and claim the promises of God. Man is depraved, corrupt and full of pride. God has also made man with a free will, and God will not step over that free will. But God is still able. "Now unto him that is able to do exceeding abundantly above all that we ask or think, according to the power that worketh in us,... " (Eph. 3:20) God's phone number: "Call unto me, and I will answer thee, and shew thee great and mighty things, which thou knowest not." (Jer. 33:3)

You may be reading this and longing in your heart for reconciliation with a loved one. Don't let your loved one destroy you. Don't let your life be wrapped up in that loved one, or loved ones. Your life is to be wrapped up with Jesus Christ. *The Lord Jesus Christ is to be your life, your love, your hope, your security and your friend.*

There are people all over the world, and especially in America, whose lives are consumed with their family and loved ones. When division happens, they are left alone, discouraged and depressed. Often they will force their way into the lives of their loved ones only to cause a greater division. I cover that in my book titled A Bad In-Law.

If you are born again, then your life should not be lived around your loved ones, but your life should be lived around your Saviour, Jesus Christ. The advantage for a Christian in regards to lack of reconciliation is that you have a life. Sometimes you will hear people say to someone, *"Get a life."* If you are saved then you have a life, and it is to be lived for Jesus Christ.

> Matt. 10:34 Think not that I am come to send peace on earth: I came not to send peace, but a sword.
>
> 35 For I am come to set a man at variance against his father, and the daughter against her mother, and the daughter in law against her mother in law.
>
> 36 And a man's foes *shall be* they of his own household.
>
> 37 He that loveth father or mother more than me is not worthy of me: and he that loveth son or daughter more than me is not worthy of me.
>
> 38 And he that taketh not his cross, and

followeth after me, is not worthy of me.
39 He that findeth his life shall lose it: and he that loseth his life for my sake shall find it.

Jesus Christ is to be your life, and you are to love Him above your family. You should not go to pieces if your family is divided. Does it hurt? Yes! Do you weep and cry? Yes! Do you carry the hurt day after day? Yes! Do you long for reconciliation? Yes! But you are to go on and serve the Lord Jesus Christ! If you are saved then you have a life, and it is to be lived for Jesus Christ, not your family.

I believe one of the reasons the Lord said that He came to set at variance a son and father, or daughter and mother, etc., is to see if He is first in your heart. If He is not first in your heart, then whatever is coming before Jesus Christ is an idol.

Many a person has made an idol out of family, and Jesus Christ has taken a back seat in their heart. "And thou shalt love the LORD thy God with all thine heart, and with all thy soul, and with all thy might." (Deut. 6:5)

Consider the following verse,

> "If any *man* come to me, and hate not his father, and mother, and wife, and children, and brethren, and sisters, yea, and his own life also, he cannot be my disciple." (Luke 14:26)

Do you really hate them or your own life? Not in

the classical sense of the word hate, but it will appear to others that you hate your family, when in fact your heart is breaking to pieces.

Just the same as you don't hate your life in the sense of you going to commit suicide. No, it's not like that. It is merely the fact that the Lord Jesus Christ is loved more than your life itself, and thus the actions that you take in order to please Him will appear to others as if you had no regard for your own person. It's not that you have no regard, it is just that Jesus Christ comes first.

"By faith Moses, when he was come to years, refused to be called the son of Pharaoh's daughter;" (Heb. 11:24) Don't you know that Moses was accused of being unthankful and even hating those who raised him, when all he was doing was obeying God. This is what you are going to have to do. You must put Jesus Christ first.

If you are saved, then keep in mind the time when you were reconciled to the Lord Jesus Christ. It was a time when all your sins were washed away and He came, wrapped His loving arms around you and brought you into the family of God. That is an eternal family.

I was at a church one time, and after the service many of the church people, as well as my wife and I, went home to the pastor's house, While there we were fellowshipping and talking about when, where and what brought each of us to the point to get saved. As we did, the pastor began to tell his testimony.

He said that he and his wife lived a hard life in

the military. He was in an upper class, or you might say, an elite soldier, but he was also drinking and living a wasted life. After getting out of the military, he and his wife settled down in the area, but the rough party life continued. His father was a saved man and a missionary thousands of miles away. Due to his father's prayers, no doubt, this pastor and his friends started studying the Bible.

This was all started when a man came on TV who drew chalk talk pictures as he preached, which caught their attention. He also was a rugged sort of preacher who placed a great emphasis on what the word of God said, not what he said. Well, this caught their attention and in the midst of parties they would sit around and discuss the word of God.

After some time, the pastor got saved and reconciled to God. One of the first things that God put on his heart was that he needed to call, or write, his father and apologize for the way he treated him. He had not been too kind to his father. He decided to write to him, which he did.

Later, after his father and he were reconciled, his father told him that the work on the mission field had been going very hard. Discouragement was high, and when he received his son's letter that he had gotten saved and also apologized to him, it greatly encouraged him to go on for Jesus Christ. The pastor and his father were reconciled.

Chapter 7
Proving

It is interesting to note that the subject of proving someone is frowned upon and you are accused of not properly forgiving, even though it is recorded many times in the Bible that God does this very thing. He proves people over and over in the word of God.

What is proving? Proving is in so many words, let's see if his actions over time match what he has said with his mouth.

There is a certain similarity between God and man in this respect. When it comes to the heart and your free will, both God and man are blind. Both are directed to view the works of the person and the spirit in which the works are done to determine genuine repentance and a genuine love towards God or the person. That is an amazing thing to think about.

Over and over in the word of God it is said that God looks on the heart. God considers the heart, but in order to do this He observes the actions of the person as well as putting them into circumstances in order to reveal their true heart. But if you and I do that we are considered wrong and unforgiving if we do such things.

Years ago, when my son was about three years old, one day I had to go do some work. At the time I was a traveling salesman, and we had to package some of the products that we sold by putting them into containers and thus getting them ready to be presented and hopefully sold. There were many colors which were very attractive and would draw a person's attention to them.

I knew this and wanted to use the opportunity to train my son not to touch. A simple thing but needful, so I left some of the product within reach of him. I told him not to touch it and I was sure he understood my command. We then proceeded to assemble the packages and products for sale. It was not long though that as we worked, my son began to touch and handle the products.

I then told him no, smacked his hands and went back to what I was doing. The other man there saw that I did not remove the product from his reach. The temptation was still present for my son to touch and handle the product. Upon seeing this, he removed the product out of the way so that my son could not reach it.

I let it go, but thought to myself, *"How is he going to learn if you remove the temptation?"* I wasn't trying to be mean, I was trying to train and thus help my son.

God will put temptation within reach of you every day of your life. Your actions prove to Him whether you love Him, and if your repentance is sincere. "He that covereth his sins shall not prosper: but whoso confesseth and forsaketh *them* shall have mercy." (Prov. 28:13)

I have heard it said that if you forgive then you are to forget. I have actually heard that preached. In this subject of reconciliation, preachers and Christians will often use our salvation as the example of perfect forgiveness, but there is a problem with this analogy. For one, when you are saved you are born again, there is the new birth. You actually become a new creature in Christ Jesus. The Bible says that, "...if any man be in Christ, he is a new creature: old things are passed away; behold, all things are become new." (2 Cor. 5:17)

Our salvation experience is not a proper place to go for a physical example of forgiveness and reconciliation. Why? Because when a person is born again there is a new relationship between you and God. You have had a new birth and you are a new creature that is a result of a supernatural act.

What's needed is an example of someone who is already saved and then turns his back on Jesus Christ, thus transgressing against the Lord Jesus Christ. That is a proper situation to illustrate from the word of God forgiveness and reconciliation, and consequently proving.

There is a perfect example in the word of God for us to study in this regard, and it is the story of Simon Peter when he denies the Lord. In this story you are given the perfect example of how the Lord deals with someone who has transgressed against him and then gets right with him and is restored.

You first have the story of Simon Peter standing around the fire.

> Matt. 26:69 ¶ Now Peter sat without in the palace: and a damsel came unto him, saying, Thou also wast with Jesus of Galilee.
>
> Matt. 26:70 But he denied before them all, saying, I know not what thou sayest.
>
> Matt. 26:71 And when he was gone out into the porch, another maid saw him, and said unto them that were there, This fellow was also with Jesus of Nazareth.
>
> Matt. 26:72 And again he denied with an oath, I do not know the man.
>
> Matt. 26:73 And after a while came unto him they that stood by, and said to Peter, Surely thou also art one of them; for thy speech bewrayeth thee.
>
> Matt. 26:74 Then began he to curse and to swear, saying, I know not the man. And immediately the cock crew.
>
> Matt. 26:75 And Peter remembered the word of Jesus, which said unto him, Before the cock crow, thou shalt deny me thrice. And he went out, and wept bitterly.

> Luke 22:61 And the Lord turned, and looked upon Peter. And Peter remembered the word of the Lord, how he had said unto him, Before the cock crow, thou shalt deny me thrice.

So here you have one of the Lord's best and main disciple, Simon Peter, and he denies the Lord. Notice in Matthew 26:72 he denies with an oath. In other words, *"I swear before God that I do not know the man."* That is a lie, and it is a lie before God. Then in Matthew 26:74 he curses and swears.

Simon Peter was a fisherman, and fisherman know how to curse and swear. Some of the old man is coming out in Simon Peter. He now curses and swears with a lie. Though not as bad, yet at the beginning of his progression verse 70 he lies by saying, "I know not what thou sayest." So now Simon Peter has sinned against his Saviour three times, and the rooster sounds off.

Upon hearing the sound of the rooster there by the fire, a memory of the Lord telling him that he was going to deny him pierces his soul. Fear, pain and sorrow all strike him at once. As the dim yellow light of the fire flickers, his face abruptly turns towards the building where Jesus Christ is being slapped and mocked. The turn of his head was so fast that it caused others to look up and to stare at him. There in the dim night Simon Peter's eyes meet with his Lord's eyes for the flash of a couple seconds. "And the Lord turned, and looked upon Peter. And Peter remembered the word of the Lord, how he had said unto him, Before the cock crow, thou shalt deny me thrice." (Luke 22:61)

A whirlwind of activity is going on. The Son of God being mocked, slapped and tortured. Peter has just denied the Lord three times. The apostle John is somewhere present as well, and many eyes are now looking upon Peter. Some of the people may even be wondering, *"What's wrong with this guy?"*

For Peter, there in the eye of the storm, everything turns into slow motion as his eyes fearfully look over to Jesus. He watches Jesus turn his head and look right at him. As their eyes meet there is a communication of ten thousand words in less than a second.

"I told you Peter that you would deny me." And with that, Peter's thoughts race as he sees the Lord, *"You knew I would do this. You told me I would deny you. Things are not out of control, you know exactly what is happening. I didn't listen to you and now I have denied you three times."* Jesus turns His head back and Peter's heart is racing faster than ever now, and as it races it begins to break. Running away from the fire and out the gate, with tears streaming down his face he collapses in a private place weeping bitter tears of repentance. *"Oh, God, I am so sorry!"*

Peter has sinned against the Lord. He has denied him and lied before God, but he has also repented over what he has done. "If we confess our sins, he is faithful and just to forgive us *our* sins, and to cleanse us from all unrighteousness." (1John 1:9)

So I ask you, was he forgiven? Yes, he was forgiven. Was he reconciled to his Lord? Yes, he was reconciled to his Lord. But there is a change in his relationship with his Lord.

Notice the following scripture:

> "But go your way, tell his disciples and Peter that he goeth before you into Galilee: there shall ye see him, as he said unto you." (Mark 16:7)

Simon Peter is no longer a disciple. The Lord does not include him with the disciples. Peter has lost his discipleship, even though he has repented and been reconciled to his Lord. Everything is not as if it never happened.

Isn't it good to know that we are saved by grace through faith? Aren't you glad that we are eternally secure? No, you are not going to lose your salvation, if you have been born again. You didn't get saved by works and you are not kept by works. But your relationship with Jesus Christ is based upon your works from your heart, along with a correct application of the true scriptures upon your daily walk.

It has now been nine or ten days since Jesus Christ resurrected from the tomb. Simon Peter has said, "I go a fishing." But they caught nothing all that night. The Lord shows up; on the lake's shore a campfire is burning, with bread and fish cooking on it. He says to them, "Come and dine."

John 21:15 ¶ So when they had dined, Jesus saith to Simon Peter, Simon, *son* of Jonas, lovest thou me more than these? He saith unto him, Yea, Lord; thou knowest that I love thee. He saith unto him, Feed my lambs.

John 21:16 He saith to him again the second time, Simon, *son* of Jonas, lovest thou me? He saith unto him, Yea, Lord; thou knowest that I love thee. He saith unto him, Feed my sheep.

John 21:17 He saith unto him the third time, Simon, son of Jonas, lovest thou me? Peter was grieved because he said unto him the third time, Lovest thou me? And he said unto him, Lord, thou knowest all things; thou knowest that I love thee. Jesus saith unto him, Feed my sheep.

John 21:18 Verily, verily, I say unto thee, When thou wast young, thou girdedst thyself, and walkedst whither thou wouldest: but when thou shalt be old, thou shalt stretch forth thy hands, and another shall gird thee, and carry *thee* whither thou wouldest not.

John 21:19 This spake he, signifying by what death he should glorify God. And when he had spoken this, he saith unto him, Follow me.

So here are the disciples and Peter sitting around the fire, having supper with the Lord, and they now know exactly who He really is. The fire flickers brightly as they dine on the fish and bread that the Lord has provided. But Simon Peter is rather quiet. His eyes stare at the ground and then into the fire and back at the ground. He has a hard time lifting his head for he is ashamed.

As the meal comes to a close and everyone is relaxed with food in their stomach, a hush seems to pass over the men. Then in front of everyone, the Lord looks at Simon Peter. His shame grows as his head drops a bit, and he hears his Lord say to him, *"Simon, son of Jonas, lovest thou me more than these?"* Peter looks up and right into the Lord's eyes. In the flash of a moment he remembered the last fire he was at when his eyes met the Lord's, and a pain seemed to shoot through his soul. *"Yes, Lord, thou knowest that I love thee."* And he did love his Lord. He wasn't lying at all. Peter's head drops back down as he stares back into the fire. He then hears Jesus tell him, *"Feed my lambs."*

The only thing heard now around the fire was the crackle and occasional pop from the wood in the fire as it burned. With each crackle and pop a few sparks would fly upward. "Yet man is born unto trouble, as the sparks fly upward." (Job 5:7)

The silence is broken again by the Lord looking at Peter and asking him again, *"Simon, son of Jonas, lovest thou me?"* The other disciples didn't say a thing, they just listened and watched. Again Simon Peter raised his head and looked at Jesus as he answered, *"Yes, Lord, thou knowest that I love thee."* A few tears seemed to drop off his cheeks as he looked back into the fire, and again he heard his Lord say, *"Feed my sheep."*

Then after a short space of time Jesus speaks again, *"Simon, son of Jonas, lovest thou me?"* That did it. Tears flowed from his eyes as he was grieved that he asked him a third time. As best as he could get it out, he said, *"Lord, you know all things; thou knowest that I love thee."* Jesus then tells him again, *"Feed my sheep."*

Notice, now that Peter has confessed him openly three times in front of everyone around a fire, the Lord begins to tell him how he is going to die. This time Peter listens intently and believes every word that the Lord speaks to him. Then he hears Jesus say to him, *"Follow me."* His discipleship has now been restored.

The lesson here has nothing to do with phileo, agape, or the other Greek word for love. The lesson here is that when you deny the Lord *it takes some proving* to get back to where you were before you had denied him. Peter was forgiven when he went out and wept bitterly, but then there came a time of proving.

Perhaps someone has broken your heart. They have betrayed your trust and trespassed against you. But thankfully you rebuked them, and they have repented and asked you to forgive them for what they have done. That is the Biblical process, and it is rare, but it does happen. So now, do you act like the trespass never happened? Well, you are not to hold it over their head or anything like that. With charity you are to move on, but with some things it will be impossible to act like nothing ever happened. Whether it is a reconciliation of a marriage, or a betrayal of a close Christian friend, or a division between a parent and their son or daughter, you must realize that it is going to take some time to work through it all.

An open wound will not heal. That is how it was when you were un-reconciled. It could never heal because it was an open wound. When a wound is closed it will heal, but it is going to take some time.

Not only that, but as we see here there is an element that you are to watch for, as John the Baptist said, "fruits meet for repentance." (Matt. 3:8) If there has been a genuine repentance then there will be fruits that will be seen. One of which is a remainder of humility and sorrow on the part of the one who betrayed you.

You are not to be haughty about it, but it is something to be aware of. To repent is to be humbled, and that condition is not one that goes away. The results of it will show in how they treat you and respect you.

The Lord does make it easy for us, and you should make it easy for them.

"Charity suffereth long, *and* is kind."

(1 Cor. 13:4)

"But the wisdom that is from above is first pure, then peaceable, gentle, and easy to be intreated, full of mercy and good fruits, without partiality, and without hypocrisy."

(James 3:17)

Chapter 8

Salvation

Dear friend, would you let me ask you one of the most important questions that you will ever be asked in this life? The question is this, *"Do you know that you are going to Heaven when you die?"*

Perhaps you say that no one knows where they are going when they die. Well, St. Peter knew that he was going to Heaven for he said that he was born again, "kept by the power of God," and that he had an incorruptible inheritance reserved in Heaven. St. John knew that he was going to Heaven for he said, "Now are we the sons of God... and we know that we shall be like Him." "These things have I written unto you that believe on the name of the Son of God; that ye may know that ye have eternal life..." (1John 5:13)

Not only did St. Peter and St. John know where they were going when they died, but St. Paul also knew for he said that he had a "desire to depart, and to be with Christ; which is far better." And of course Jesus Christ said, "I go unto my Father."

All of these men, as well as the Son of God, knew where they were going when they died. If they knew, you can know also. In the Bible St. John wrote again, "These things have I written unto you that believe on the name of the Son of God; that ye may know that ye have eternal life..." (1 Jn 5:13)

Do you know that you have eternal life? Do you know that you are going to Heaven when you die?

Let me start at the very beginning. The person you are going to have to deal with is called, "the Word," and He is the Creator of all things.

> John 1:1 In the beginning was the Word, and the Word was with God, and the Word was God.
>
> 2 The same was in the beginning with God.
>
> 3 All things were made by him; and without him was not any thing made that was made. 4 In him was life; and the life was the light of men.

He is also righteous. In Heaven they worship Him.

> Rev. 4:8 And the four beasts had each of them six wings about *him*; and *they were* full of eyes within: and they rest not day and night, saying, Holy, holy, holy, Lord

God Almighty, which was, and is, and is to come.

His name is the Son of God, the Lord Jesus Christ.

"But unto the Son *he saith*, Thy throne, O God, *is* for ever and ever: a sceptre of righteousness *is* the sceptre of thy kingdom." (Heb. 1:8)

The Lord Jesus Christ is Holy. That means He has never sinned one time. There is no spot nor blemish in the Lord Jesus Christ. He is absolutely perfect. Along with that, Heaven is also perfect. It is a place of joy, happiness, light, and righteousness. In Heaven:

Rev. 21:4 And God shall wipe away all tears from their eyes; and there shall be no more death, neither sorrow, nor crying, neither shall there be any more pain: for the former things are passed away.

5 And he that sat upon the throne said, Behold, I make all things new. And he said unto me, Write: for these words are true and faithful.

This is just a glimpse of Heaven but it gives a glimpse of a place where it can honestly be written as an epigraph, *"...and they lived happily ever after."* Doesn't that sound like a place you would like to spend eternity in?

Heaven is beautiful because the God of Heaven

is holy, the place called Heaven is holy, and the people of Heaven are holy. My desire in writing this is to tell you how you can know when you die you will make it to this beautiful place called Heaven. Then it can be written of you, he or she lived happily ever after.

This brings us to the subject of holiness. Are you holy? Are you righteous? Are you a good person? To answer the first two questions I would think it would be easy to answer, *"No."* You are not holy, and you are not righteous. But maybe your answer to the third question is, *"Yes."* You might say that you are a good person. You're nice to others and try to help folks when you can. That is a good thing.

When it comes to holiness though, how do we judge what is holy? How do we know what holiness is? To answer these two questions we must go back in time about 3500 years to a mountain in Arabia. It is a mountain called Mt. Sinai. On that mountain is a man called Moses. The Lord God has called him there, and camped below in the plain is a nation God has called out of Egypt named Israel.

The top of that mountain can be seen today in 2017. It is in Arabia and has been burnt black, and is a reminder of the event that I am about to tell you of.

Moses went up onto the mount, and God came down in fire on the top of that mount and gave Moses the Ten Commandments. These Ten Commandments are a glimpse of holiness, or should I say, the standard by which holiness is judged. I am going to use only four of the ten and let's see how you measure up to holiness.

1. Ex. 20:7 Thou shalt not take the name of the LORD thy God in vain; for the LORD will not hold him guiltless that taketh his name in vain.

This is the third commandment. To take the Lord's name in vain is called blasphemy and it is very serious. Have you ever taken the Lord's name in vain? In other words have you ever said, *"Oh my God,"* or *"Jesus Christ,"* or *"Lord God Almighty,"* or just *"Jesus?"*

Have you ever said any of these in vain, or other variations? How many times in your life have you taken His name in vain? In vain would mean that you just said His name without using it in a sentence, thus in vain. Since this is called blasphemy, then you would be called a blasphemer.

If you have broken this commandment then you are a *blasphemer*.

2. Ex. 20:15 Thou shalt not steal.

This is the eighth commandment. Have you ever stolen anything in your life? Stop and think about this. Have you ever, without permission, downloaded any music, or anything that was copyrighted? Have you ever taken something that was not yours? Size does not matter. From a piece of candy to millions of dollars, have you ever stolen something?

It doesn't matter what religion you are, for these laws are written on your heart. You know instinctively that it is wrong to take something that is not yours.

What does God call someone who steals? They are called a *thief*. So then if you have stolen anything you are a thief. You are guilty of breaking God's law when He wrote, "Thou shalt not steal."

If you have broken both of these commandments, then you are a blasphemer and a thief. Keep in mind this is only two of the ten commandments.

3. Ex. 20:14 Thou shalt not commit adultery.

This is to have sex with someone who is not your spouse, thus it is to have sex outside of marriage.

Jesus, who was God manifest in the flesh, went even farther and stated, Matt. 5:28 "But I say unto you, That whosoever looketh on a woman to lust after her hath committed adultery with her already in his heart."

Adultery is now committed in your heart by looking on someone and lusting after them sexually, as well as the physical act of fornicating with someone. Fornication is what it is called when sex is committed outside of marriage. This would include Sodomy. Have you ever done that?

If you have, even if just once, then you are an adulterer, or could also be called a fornicator. If you have broken all three of these commandments then you are a blasphemer, thief and a fornicator.

4. Matt. 19:18 "...Thou shalt not bear false witness."

Also known as, "Thou shalt not lie."

Have you ever told a lie? To speak a false witness is to tell a lie. A witness tells what he or she knows. To be a false witness is to not speak or tell the truth about what you know. Have you ever done that? How many times have you done that in your life? 1 time? 10? 100? 1000? Etc.?

A person who tells lies, is called a *liar*. Then you are a liar.

If you have transgressed all four of these commandments then you are a *blasphemer, a thief, a fornicator and a liar*. Do you think God will allow you into Heaven? What kind of place would Heaven be if God allowed blasphemers, thieves, fornicators and liars into it? I'll tell you, it wouldn't be a holy place, and it wouldn't be Heaven.

With just four out of ten commandments, we have had a glimpse of holiness. The Bible states, "Wherefore the law is holy, and the commandment holy, and just, and good." Rom. 7:12 "...but I am carnal, sold under sin." Rom. 7:14

The truth of the matter is that you are not holy, nor are you even good, and neither am I. We all are sinners and have broken God's commandments.

The Bible says,

> 1Cor. 6:9 Know ye not that the unrighteous shall not inherit the kingdom of God? Be not deceived: neither fornicators, nor idolaters, nor adulterers, nor effeminate, nor abusers of themselves

with mankind,

10 Nor thieves, nor covetous, nor drunkards, nor revilers, nor extortioners, shall inherit the kingdom of God.

Rev. 21:8 But the fearful, and unbelieving, and the abominable, and murderers, and whoremongers, and sorcerers, and idolaters, and all liars, shall have their part in the lake which burneth with fire and brimstone: which is the second death.

Rev. 20:14 And death and hell were cast into the lake of fire. This is the second death.

15 And whosoever was not found written in the book of life was cast into the lake of fire.

If you die right now, according to the word of God, where will you go? Have you ever told a lie? Then you are a liar and according to the Bible you will go to the lake of fire.

Is that where you want to go when you die? If you are in your right mind then you do not want to end up in the Lake of Fire for all eternity.

Is there a way to be saved from going to Hell? If you have been honest with yourself about those four commandments, then you know that you have broken at least one of them. The Bible says, For whosoever shall keep the whole law, and yet offend in one *point*, he is guilty of all. James 2:10

Then according to the word of God you are guilty of breaking God's law and thus unable of your own self to enter Heaven.

In your present condition you will one day stand before your Creator and Judge who will pronounce the judgement, *"Guilty!"* The punishment for you is that you will be cast into Hell and then later cast into the Lake of Fire. That is what you deserve, and that is what I deserve as well, but this is where the good news begins.

Good News

Jesus Christ was God manifest in the flesh. That means Jesus Christ was fully God. He came to this earth being born of the virgin Mary, and became a man. While on this earth He never broke God's law one time. Jesus Christ lived a perfect life according to His law. Jesus Christ is Holy. How do I know this? Because after He was crucified on the cross, our Lord arose from the dead after spending three days and three nights in the heart of the earth.

If Jesus Christ had sinned one time, then He never would have been able to rise from the dead. He would have been just like you and me. But He did rise from the dead and was seen by over 500 people after He arose from the dead.

Jesus Christ saw you long before you were ever around. He saw you and He loved you.

> For God so loved the world, that he gave his only begotten Son, that whosoever

> believeth in him should not perish, but
> have everlasting life. John 3:16

God gave his Son; how? He gave him when Jesus died on the cross as the sacrifice for your sins. Jesus Christ took the punishment of your sins upon Himself, and shed His blood as the perfect payment for your sins. The sins that you committed when you transgressed those commandments have all been paid for.

> Rom. 5:6 For when we were yet without strength, in due time Christ died for the ungodly.
> 7 For scarcely for a righteous man will one die: yet peradventure for a good man some would even dare to die.
> 8 But God commendeth his love toward us, in that, while we were yet sinners, Christ died for us.
> 9 Much more then, being now justified by his blood, we shall be saved from wrath through him.

While you were a sinner, Jesus Christ loved you and died for you on the cross. He also shed His blood as the payment for your sins, but you must pick up the payment. "For the wages of sin *is* death; but the gift of God *is* eternal life through Jesus Christ our Lord." (Rom. 6:23)

Wages are given as payment for something that you have worked for. Those commandments that you have broken have earned you death. That is your payment, that is what you have worked for.

A gift is something that you do not work for. A gift is given free of charge after the giver worked to purchase it or to make it. The gift that I am writing about here is eternal life. Do you want to live forever? Do you want to go to Heaven when you die? It is a free gift, but there is one catch. You must receive the Lord Jesus Christ in order to obtain eternal life.

Eternal life is not obtained through baptism, church membership, getting rid of bad karma, or any other works. It is obtained through our Lord Jesus Christ. He is the One that paid the price. You must receive Jesus Christ as your very own personal Saviour.

> John 1:10 He was in the world, and the world was made by him, and the world knew him not.
>
> 11 He came unto his own, and his own received him not.
>
> 12 But as many as received him, to them gave he power to become the sons of God, *even* to them that believe on his name:
>
> 13 Which were born, not of blood, nor of the will of the flesh, nor of the will of man, but of God.

So how do you receive Jesus Christ? If you can't see Him, feel Him or touch Him, how can you receive Him? "For whosoever shall call upon the name of the Lord shall be saved." (Rom. 10:13)

You must pray and ask Jesus Christ to forgive you of your sins; to wash you from your sins in His own blood; and ask Him to come into your heart and save you from your sins. "And from Jesus Christ, *who is* the faithful witness, *and* the first begotten of the dead, and the prince of the kings of the earth. Unto him that loved us, and washed us from our sins in his own blood." (Rev. 1:5)

Summary:

1. You have broken God's Holy Commands. Blasphemer, Thief, Fornicator or Liar - Guilty! Headed for the Lake of Fire.

2. Jesus Christ died for your sins, was buried and three days later arose from the grave proving that He was God manifest in the flesh. He paid for all of your sins. Your ticket to Heaven is all paid for, now you must receive Jesus Christ into your heart in order to claim the payment for your sins.

3. You must call upon the Lord Jesus Christ to forgive you of your sins and to wash you in His blood. You must ask the Lord Jesus Christ to come into your heart and save you.

Here is a simple prayer to pray. Remember though, that by faith in what God said, you are talking to Jesus Christ from your heart. Reciting this prayer will not save you. You must realize that you are talking to your Saviour, Jesus Christ. He is the One you need to forgive you and to save you. He promised to save you if you call upon His name and God cannot lie. The best way you know how pray this prayer out loud. Talk to the Lord out loud.

Dear Lord Jesus Christ. I come to you as a sinner who has broken your commandments. I am guilty. I believe you died on the cross and paid for my sins. Please forgive me of my sins. Please wash me throughly in your blood. And dear Jesus, please come into my heart and save me. I don't want to go to the Lake of Fire. Thank you for dying for me on the cross and thank you for saving me. In your name, Lord Jesus, I ask these things, Amen.

If you prayed a prayer like that one and meant it, then according to the word of God you are saved from eternal damnation. I now ask you, "Where are you now going when you die?"

> Rom. 10:13 For whosoever shall call upon the name of the Lord shall be saved.

> John 6:37 All that the Father giveth me shall come to me; and him that cometh to me I will in no wise cast out.

These are both prescious promises from the word of God.

Made in the USA
Columbia, SC
09 May 2017